Back Roads of Washington

Rt. 1 Box 444
Geo. L. Yarnell

Seen near
BZ Corners,
Klickitat County

Books by Earl Thollander

BACK ROADS OF NEW ENGLAND
BACK ROADS OF OREGON
BACK ROADS OF WASHINGTON
BACK ROADS OF CALIFORNIA
BACK ROADS OF TEXAS
BACK ROADS OF ARIZONA
BARNS OF CALIFORNIA

Farm on Lopez Island,
San Juan County

Back Roads of Washington

by Earl Thollander

Clarkson N. Potter, Inc./Publishers NEW YORK
DISTRIBUTED BY CROWN PUBLISHERS, INC.

I dedicate this book
to Diana Klemin

Front cover: The old lighthouse
at Marrowstone Point,
Jefferson County

Copyright © 1981 by Earl Thollander

All rights reserved. No part of this book may be reproduced or
utilized in any form or by any means, electronic or mechanical,
including photocopying, recording, or by any information stor-
age and retrieval system, without permission in writing from
the publisher.

Inquiries should be addressed to Clarkson N. Potter, Inc.,
One Park Avenue, New York, New York 10016

Printed in the United States of America

Published simultaneously in Canada by General Publishing
Company Limited

Library of Congress Cataloging in Publication Data

Thollander, Earl.
  Back roads of Washington.

  1. Washington (State)—Description and travel—1951-
—Guide-books. 2. Automobiles—Road guides—Washington
(State) 3. Washington (State)—History, Local. I. Title.
F889.3.T48   1981   917.970443   81-5128
ISBN: 0-517-542692 (cloth)   AACR2
ISBN: 0-517-542706 (paper)

10 9 8 7 6 5 4 3 2 1

First Edition

Grain elevator
at Marlin,
Grant County

Contents

Back Roads of Southwestern Washington

Back Roads of Northwestern Washington

Back Roads of Northeastern Washington

Map legend

._____5.6_____. distance in miles between dots

→ → → my route (which may be reversed should you desire)

▲ campgrounds
■ towns and cities
▭ dams
.... rivers, lakes, ferry routes
□ special place
✕ my sketching place
⛪ church
⊼ picnic grounds
⊡ cemetery
△ mountains
⌂ buildings

NORTH is always toward the top of the page

Back Roads of Southeastern Washington

Yellow
Dandelion

Sketching in Oysterville,
Pacific County

Foreword

Bob Meadows knocked on the door of our cottage and came in before we could answer. "Hey," he said, "there's an artist fellow sittin' out there in the field, just a-drawin' away. I'd sure like to see what he'd do if one of them great big b'ars come up and looked over his shoulder."

As it happens, there are no great big b'ars around Oysterville; ours are middle-sized fellows, though fearsome enough at that. But even if a Kodiak brown bear in all its terrible majesty came visiting, I know what Earl Thollander would do: He would make a place for it in his drawing.

He was sitting out there that rainy day because of me. I had written a book, *Oysterville: Roads to Grandpa's Village,* and Earl had agreed to pretty up the pages with sketches of local sights, animate and inanimate—snipe, oyster shells, falling-down fences, and so on. The way he does.

The way he does is a thing to marvel at. For years, Earl Thollander has been exploring the back roads of this nation, sketching as he goes. His means of transportation is a 1972 Chevrolet pickup truck that serves as both studio and bedroom. At intervals he parks off the road, gets out, and begins to draw. You may have seen him sitting on a rail fence, with his pad in his lap, or leaning forward in a canvas folding chair in a field, as on that day in Oysterville. To find the best vantage point, he sometimes climbs into the branches of a tree or onto the roof of a farmhouse.

Each expedition adds a new installment to a unique pictorial chronicle of America. It is an America invisible from superhighways and absent from headlines. In the America recorded by Earl Thollander you will still find covered bridges, steepled country churches, and barns bursting with hay. You can still pause to marvel over a half-opened jonquil or the cemented nest of a mud swallow. It is an America that has never gone away, but that was forgotten for a while. Now that we are seeking it again, Earl Thollander is pointing out the way.

Should the day come, God forbid, when the last covered bridge and steepled church have vanished, Thollander's elegant drawings will remain as testimony—part of the heritage that they record.

You may fairly accuse me of chauvinism when I say that I admire *Back Roads of Washington* even more than its predecessors. I am, after all, Washingtonian by birth and rearing. But I am right. The two-page drawing of Oysterville is sufficient by itself to make this book immortal.

Willard R. Espy

Oysterville, Washington
January 1981

Preface

Seeing Washington at a leisurely pace,
following where its back roads lead me,
there is time to meet people, to meditate on
history, to take the measure of the land.
I feel close to the earth — its forests, farms,
meadows, wild birds, animals —
and joyful and at peace with man.

Snowbush,
Spokane County

Author's Note

Back Roads of Washington is a nonhighway travel guide through areas of interest and beauty. Each of the book's four parts begins with a sectional map. These will help you locate the back roads on larger maps of Washington State that are available at no charge from many sources, including travel services, chambers of commerce, tourist bureaus, and automobile clubs. Localized maps for all the roads throughout will guide you on specific trips. Unless otherwise indicated, the North Pole is toward the top of the page. Arrows trace my direction of travel, although the routes can easily be reversed. Maps are not to scale because the roads are of varying lengths; however, the mileage notations will provide a sense of their distance. Your odometer will not measure distance exactly the same as mine, but the differences should not be too great. County maps purchased from the Washington State Highway Commission, Highway Administration Building, Olympia, Washington 98504, were essential to me in following the back roads. I also purchased maps at ranger stations when entering forest preserves.

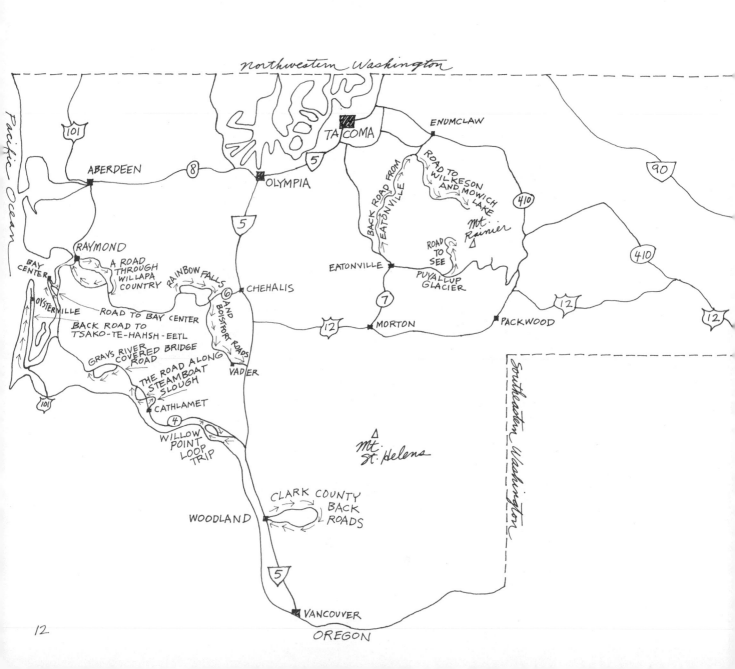

Northwestern Washington

Pacific Ocean

101

ABERDEEN — 8 — OLYMPIA

TACOMA

ENUMCLAW

90

5

5

RAYMOND

A ROAD THROUGH WILLAPA COUNTRY

BAY CENTER

OYSTERVILLE

ROAD TO BAY CENTER

BACK ROAD TO TSAKO-TE-HAHSH-EETL

GRAYS RIVER COVERED BRIDGE ROAD

THE ROAD ALONG STEAMBOAT SLOUGH

RAINBOW FALLS

6 AND BOISTFORT ROADS

CHEHALIS

BACK ROAD FROM EATONVILLE

ROAD TO WILKESON AND MOWICH LAKE

410

Mt. Rainier

410

ROAD TO SEE

EATONVILLE

PUYALLUP GLACIER

7

12

MORTON

PACKWOOD

12

12

VADER

Mt. St. Helens

101

CATHLAMET

4

WILLOW POINT LOOP TRIP

CLARK COUNTY BACK ROADS

WOODLAND

Southeastern Washington

5

VANCOUVER

OREGON

Southwestern Washington

I recall the big
foreign-bound cargo
ships navigating the
bends of the Columbia
River; a cool, misty
evening while camping
at Fort Canby
State Park; a fresh
fish dinner
(perhaps the best
I've ever had)
at South Bend;
snow-topped Mount
Rainier glistening in
the sunshine, and
foxglove blossoming
six feet tall.

Foxglove,
Pierce County

Clark County back roads

The road takes me across
the Lewis River and from
time to time touches the
river as it winds past
farms, barns, meadows,
and forest land.
   The 1876 gristmill at
Cedar Creek was
sturdily built, and
   stands to this day
for people to enjoy.
This custom mill, where
local farmers brought
their wheat, rye, and
buckwheat to be ground,
is a fascinating souvenir
of Washington's early
agricultural history.

Gristmill, 1876,
Clark County

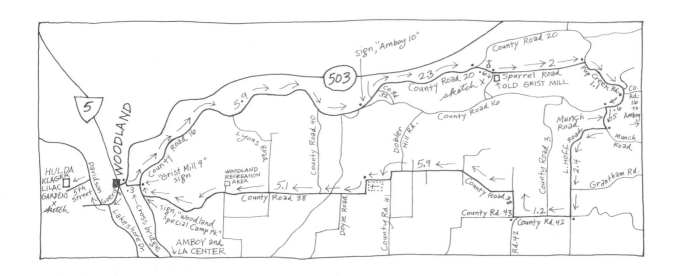

The road to Hulda Klager's house

There are exotic trees and flowers in abundance
all around the house of the "Lilac Lady," hybridizer
Hulda Klager, in Woodland. The Woodland
Federated Garden Club saved the old house
and gardens from the bulldozers when she died
in 1960 at the age of ninety-six, and the
garden club continues to maintain them.
Go anytime, but the best season is
spring, when you will see the many Klager
varieties of lilacs and experience the charm
of Hulda's house and garden at its peak.
The doll, in my picture from the Klager home,
is nicely handmade of lisle cotton stocking
material. Grace Davis's rocker dates
from about 1880.

Grace Davis's rocker
circa 1880, Hulda Klager
House, Woodland,
Cowlitz County

17

Willow Grove loop trip along the Columbia River

While riding atop dikes one gets views of
pastureland, grazing cows, barns, fishing boats,
log floats, and, of course, the Columbia River
with its big cargo ship traffic on the opposite
shore. The wooded hills of Oregon are a
backdrop. The 1,200-mile-long Columbia is one
of the largest rivers in the world, draining an
area of 257,000 square miles. I will view its
greatness many more times in my back road
journey through Washington State.

The Columbia River,
Cowlitz County

Old pilings,
Columbia River,
Wahkiakum County

TO CATHLAMET   Taylor Sands
                Road   ↑ CASTLE
   ④   ROCK
sketch ✕
                        2.9
              2.8
         Willow Grove Road
           •Willow Grove Rd   Mt. Solo Road
Columbia   1.7   1.8
                                    Barlow
River   Point Road   5.5
                                Mt. Solo Road
                                            ④
                                           ④32   LONGVIEW

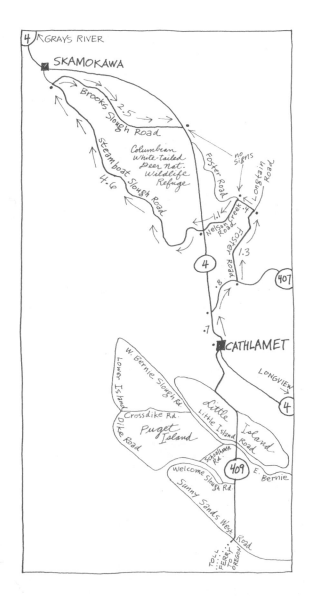

The road along Steamboat Slough

    I travel along dike roads past farms and waterways and am struck by the bouquets of wild grass, flowers, and sometimes young trees that grow from the tops of old pilings. Many are quite decorative, as if specially arranged for the delectation of travelers on back roads.

    On Puget Island, south of Cathlamet, are other dike roads. A toll ferry from the island crosses the Columbia River into Oregon.

Grays River Covered Bridge road

    This trip is through green meadows and forest
land with views of Grays River, farms, barns, and cows.
The bridge was built in 1905 and is the only covered
bridge in Washington still in use by cars.   I make
my drawing and proceed across it and along a
road lined with wild flowers.

Grays River Covered Bridge,
Wahkiakum County

23

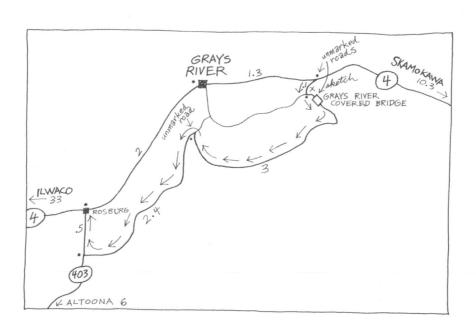

GRAYS RIVER   1.3   unmarked roads

SKAMOKAWA
④   10.3

sketch

GRAYS RIVER
COVERED BRIDGE

unmarked road

2

3

ILWACO
← 33

④   ■ ROSBURG

.5   2.4

(403)

← ALTOONA 6

*Wild blackberry,
Pacific County*

Back road to Tsako-te-hahsh-eetl

Foliage here is so dense, at times
the road seems walled with green.
There are some cranberry bogs,
a lovely old hillside cemetery
nestled in lush green forest and,
at Nahcotta, heaps of Willapa Bay
oyster shells. Oysterville, called
by Indians Tsako-te-hahsh-eetl
(Land of the Red-top Grass and Home of
the Woodpecker), is a charming
hamlet where descendants of the
co-founder, R.H. Espy, still live.
   In my drawing you see the
1869 W.W. Little house and the
Oysterville Church, its orange
and white roof topped by a
gleaming gold ball. A venerable
organ stands on each side of
   the interior of the church —
no doubt producing music as
rich as a stereo hi-fi.
   An immersion tank below
the floor for baptisms, I was
told, was used only once,
because no drain had
   been installed.
   I observe what I call
"hesitation light" in Oysterville.
Being near the coast and most
often cloudy, the light suddenly
brightens or fades, depending
upon the intensity of
changing cloud layers.

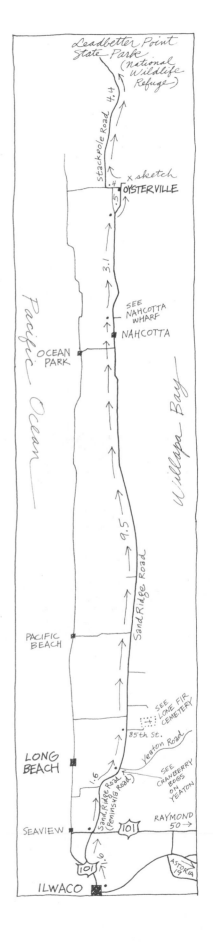

26

Oysterville,
Pacific County

27

The road to Bay Center

Harry Bochau, pronounced Bó-haw, once owned this house in the quiet little fishing and oyster town of Bay Center. I talked to his son, who has since sold it, and learned that the old house had been called "The Château." Harry planted the monkey puzzle tree, a tall Chilean evergreen; I had also seen one at the Hulda Klager lilac gardens. Its intertwined branches and stiff sharp-pointed leaves are a challenge to draw.

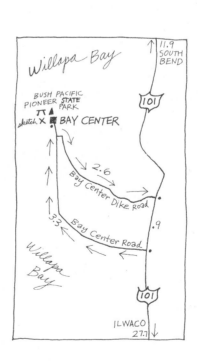

The Château,
Bay Center,
Pacific County

a road through Willapa country

This is a rolling, verdant landscape of forest and farms— a country for lumbering and dairies. I sketch the Willow River Dairy with its big 1910 barn and the milk parlor on the left, the old 1889 house, and the railroad bridge.

The owner of the farm bicycles out to meet me while I am sketching. She tells me of the many demanding routines that must be maintained on a dairy farm, in addition to the obvious daily necessity of milking the cows. Later I lunch at a hillside cemetery and take in a grand view of Willapa Valley.

Willow River Dairy, 1889,
Pacific County

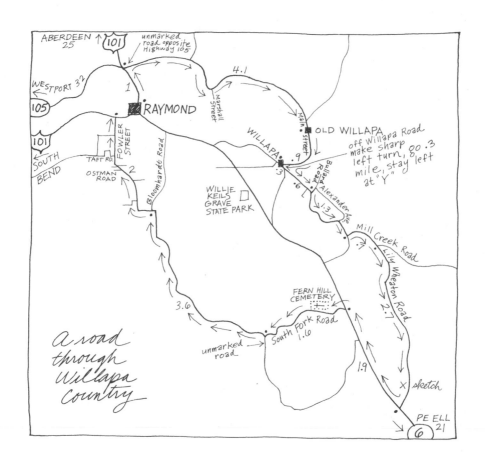

ABERDEEN ↑ 25 [101]
unmarked road opposite Highway 105

WESTPORT 32
[105]
1

[101]
SOUTH BEND

4.1

Marshall Street

RAYMOND

FOWLER STREET
TAFT RD.
OSTMAN ROAD
2

Bloomhardt Road

WILLIE KEILS GRAVE STATE PARK

WILLAPA
.9
.3
.6

Main Street

OLD WILLAPA
off Willapa Road make sharp left turn, go .3 mile, stay left at "Y"

Ballard Alexander Ave. Road
1.3

Mill Creek Road
Lily Wheaton Road
2.7

.7

FERN HILL CEMETERY

3.6

unmarked road
South Fork Road 1.6

1.9

X sketch

PE ELL 21
6

a road through Willapa Country

Rainbow Falls and Boistfort roads

Scenes along the road from Rainbow Falls State Park include an old covered railroad bridge (now without train rails), forest, farms, and glimpses of the Chehalis River. Past Boistfort the road runs through glorious farm country—meadows green with crops of corn, hay, and peas.

Wildwood Dairy features a tall, dark blue silo. The young owner left his Dairy Science course at college to run this 170-acre farm.

Chandler Road 3.4 ⊞

Elk Creek Rd.
← Stevens Rd. Kobe Road

Toppelt Rd. 1.1 Stevens Road 1.4 .8 ⛺ ▲ Leudinghaus Road 3.4 Meskill Road

RAINBOW FALLS STATE PARK

OLD RAILROAD BRIDGE ⑥ Ceres Hill 3 CHEHALIS 9 → ⑥

PE ELL 5.5 Ceres Hill Road 3 (ARCHED BRIDGE) Curtis Hill Road

WHITE RD. .2 BOISTFORT RD.

Noon Hill Road King Road

7.4 Hubbard Road

MacDonald Road

BOISTFORT

PE ELL

14.4

X sketch

Canada
Thistle,
Lewis
County

CHEHALIS 24

Wildwood Road CHEHALIS

RYDERWOOD ↓ ⑤⓪⑥

33

34   Wildwood Dairy, Lewis County

35

Puyallup Glacier,
Mt. Rainier, Pierce County

The back road to see Puyallup and Tahoma glaciers

There are two confused fawns on the road, not knowing which way to go to escape my oncoming vehicle. They finally bolt off through Douglas fir, western hemlock, and red cedar forest, and are soon hidden among vine maple, moss and fern. At the viewpoint of Puyallup Glacier, its river pounds down the mountain with rock-crushing force, yet on the banks close by, in all tranquility, grow dainty columbine, daisies, penstemon, tiger lily, cow parsnip, lungwort, and other wild flowers.

The Tahoma Glacier, which I sketch on the return trip, plays hide-and-seek with me, great mists and clouds constantly rearranging themselves on the mountain. Outsized horseflies circle, keeping up a constant hum, but they do not bite.

Majestic Mount Rainier with its 27 glaciers and 14,410-foot height is stunning and awe-inspiring—what a mountain!

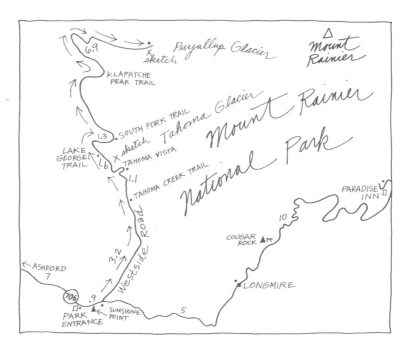

Tahoma Glacier,
Mt. Rainier,
Pierce County

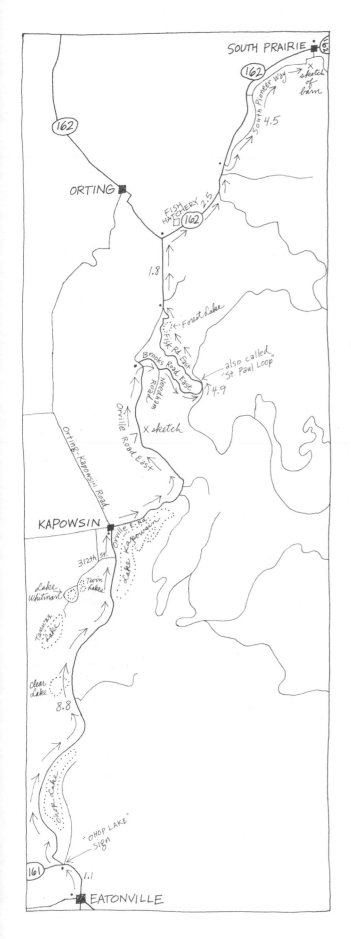

SOUTH PRAIRIE

162

South Pioneer Way

X sketch of barn

4.5

162

ORTING

FISH HATCHERY 162

2.5

1.8

← Forest Lake

Fisk Rd East

Brooks Road East

Needham Road

also called "St. Paul Loop"

4.9

Orville Road East

X sketch

Orville E. Rd.

Lake Kapowsin

KAPOWSIN

Orting-Kapowsin Road

312th St.

Lake Whitman

Twin Lakes

Tanwax Lake

clear Lake

8.8

Ohop Lake

"OHOP LAKE" sign

161

1.1

EATONVILLE

Back road from Eatonville

The road passes Ohop
Lake through the lush meadow
and farm landscape of Ohop
Valley to Kopowsin Lake
and South Prairie town.
I stop along the way at
the fish hatchery to watch
tiny salmon leaping about.
One leaps ¡too far!
It jumps onto a gravel
path and I return it to the
water. Near South Prairie
I draw the Winters barn.
Mrs. Winters tells people
who look for the farm,
"watch for the ugliest barn!"
I equip myself with a
can of dog repellent, which
Mrs. Winters gives to me in
case the big ram should come
close and lower his head in
my direction. "Don't turn
your back on him," she
cautions. The formidable
ram chews a bit on my
folding chair while I sit
in the meadow and sketch,
but luckily that is all.

Seen on the road to South Prairie, Pierce County

42

Winters Barn,
near South Prairie, Pierce County

The road to Wilkeson and Mowich Lake

The early settlers of Wilkeson, a town rimmed by conifer forest, were the immigrants who worked in local coal mines. Mining declined in the area around 1912, but in 1883 the nearby Carbonado mines were the second largest in Washington. The nicely restored Orthodox church, topped with a pale blue onion dome, is the oldest of its kind in Washington. It is located on Long Street. If you drive north to Short Street, then east to Cothery Street, you will see a castle.

Holy Trinity Orthodox Church, 1900,
Wilkeson, Pierce County

It was constructed by a Wilkeson carpenter who dreamed of building and living in his own castle. The owner isn't home when I visit, but I talk to his neighbor through a screen door as he watches television. "I don't mind a castle going up next door," he comments in good cheer.

I then drive to glacially formed Mowich Lake, which is surrounded by high-ridged peaks and trails that invite investigation.

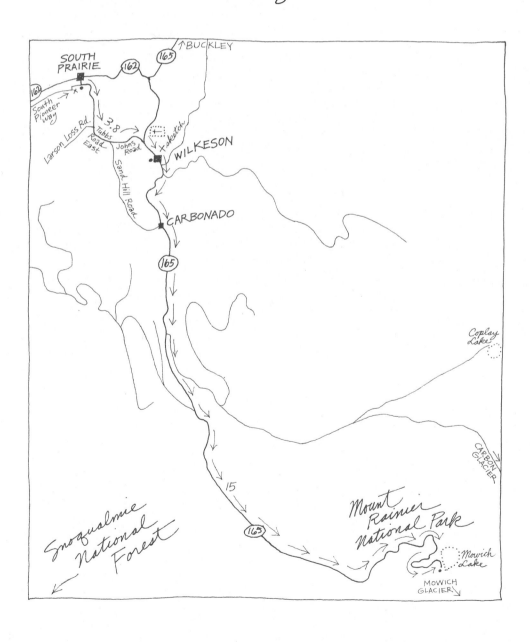

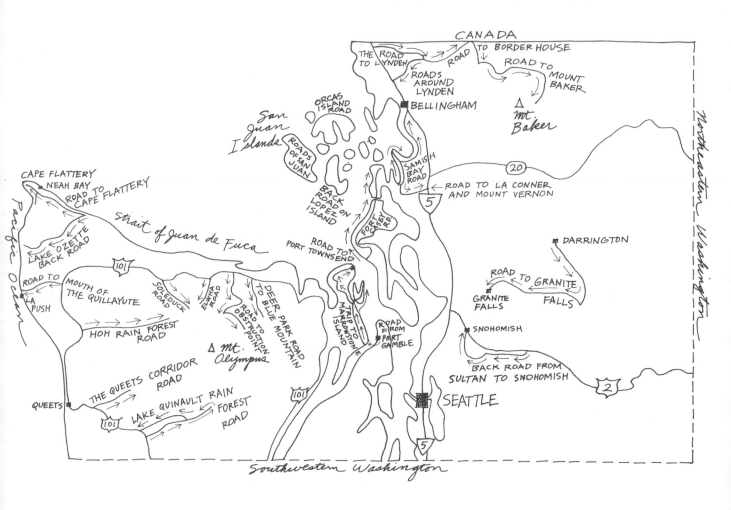

CANADA

THE ROAD TO LYNDEN

ROAD TO BORDER HOUSE

ROADS AROUND LYNDEN

ROAD TO MOUNT BAKER

ORCAS ISLAND ROAD

△ mt. Baker

BELLINGHAM

San Juan Islands

ROADS OF SAN JUAN

SAMISH BAY ROAD

20

ROAD TO LA CONNER AND MOUNT VERNON

5

BACK ROAD ON LOPEZ ISLAND

CAPE FLATTERY

NEAH BAY

ROAD TO CAPE FLATTERY

Northeastern Washington

FORT CASEY RD.

DARRINGTON

Strait of Juan de Fuca

Pacific Ocean

LAKE OZETTE BACK ROAD

ROAD TO PORT TOWNSEND

ROAD TO LA PUSH

101

MOUTH OF THE QUILLAYUTE

SOLEDUCK ROAD

ELWHA ROAD

ROAD TO OBSTRUCTION POINT

DEER PARK ROAD TO BLUE MOUNTAIN

ROAD TO GRANITE FALLS

GRANITE FALLS

HOH RAIN FOREST ROAD

△ mt. Olympus

TRIP TO MARROWSTONE ISLAND

ROAD FROM PORT GAMBLE

SNOHOMISH

THE QUEETS CORRIDOR ROAD

101

BACK ROAD FROM SULTAN TO SNOHOMISH

2

QUEETS

101

LAKE QUINAULT RAIN FOREST ROAD

SEATTLE

5

Southwestern Washington

Northwestern Washington

I recall the rich greenness of the Olympic forest, the alpine glory of Mount Olympus, a view of Tatoosh Island off Cape Flattery bathed in sunshine, the fun of ferryboat rides among the San Juans, the neatly arranged farms of the descendants of the early Dutch settlers near Lynden, and uncooperative Mount Baker that would not come out of its cloud cover so I could draw it.

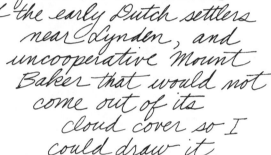

Fireweed, Snohomish County

Lake Quinault rain forest road

Hemlock, alder, cedar, maple, and fir
are all draped with moss. Soft light
filters to a forest floor blanketed
with fern and oxalis. I ride on a good
gravel road that is narrow in spots
and has obviously been planned with
the beauty of the landscape in mind
rather than speed. At the end of the
road foot trails begin beside clear,
rushing Grave Creek.

Forest road,
Olympic National Park,
Grays and Jefferson Counties

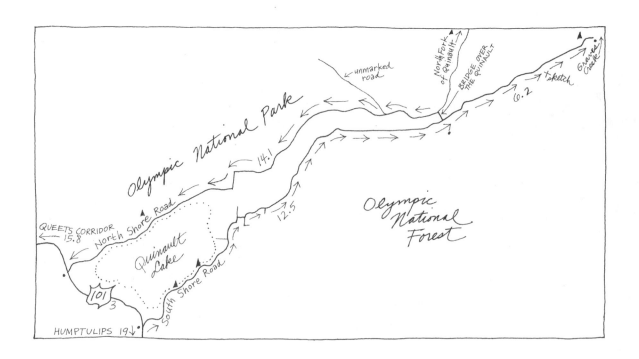

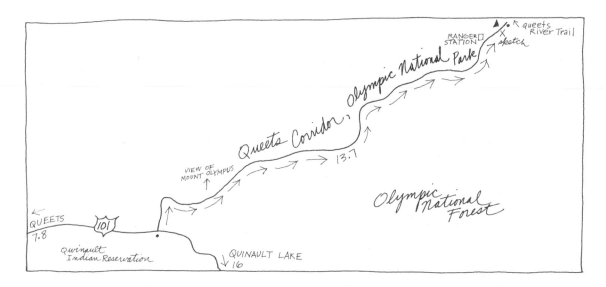

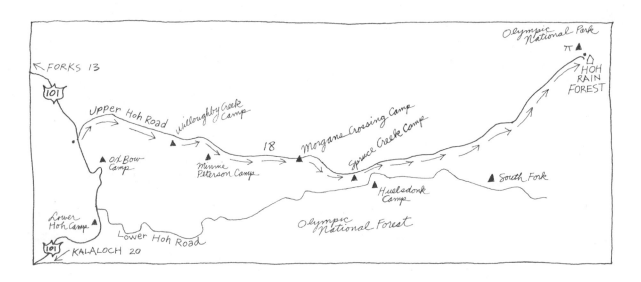

The Queets Corridor road

The road following Queets River runs through a deep rain forest. At the end of the corridor I have a fine view of the Queets. A sign at the beginning of a hike from here states, "You must ford the Queets River first before taking the trail. It is wide and rocky and you must choose a good spot since it changes from year to year. After a rainfall it might be too difficult to ford."

Trails go up the Queets River or branch off along Tshletshy Creek to the North Fork of the Quinault River.

The road to Hoh Rain Forest is another that must be experienced. At Hoh there are short walks one can take to see epiphytes (air plants) in profusion and thick draperies of club moss, giant Sitka spruce, hemlock, fir, red cedar, and red alder. All this green glory is supported by about 142 inches of rain each year in the Hoh Valley.

Tall Lungwort, Jefferson County

Rain forest,
Queets Corridor,
Jefferson County

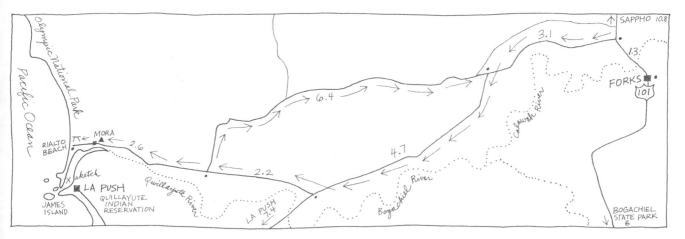

The road to the mouth of the Quillayute

It is a fast back road through the forest to the beach opposite La Push at the mouth of the Quillayute. The village looks inviting from the Rialto Beach side, near Mora. Once there, however, it isn't quite as picturesque, although the fishing boats and wharf activity lend some excitement to the town. I sketch James Island across the Quillayute and a fishing boat bringing in its catch.

Mora Beach has naturalist walks and trails leading to other beaches, which are separated by bold, rocky headlands.

Lake Ozette back road

No road at all reached Ozette until about 1930.. The Scandinavians who homesteaded the area had to pack in along the Hoko River trail. Now the road follows the Hoko River and Big River to tranquil Lake Ozette. Here trail heads begin to Sand Point and to Cape Alava. Excavations are being made just north of the cape, where an Ozette Indian village was buried by mud some four hundred years ago.

Lake Ozette, Clallam County

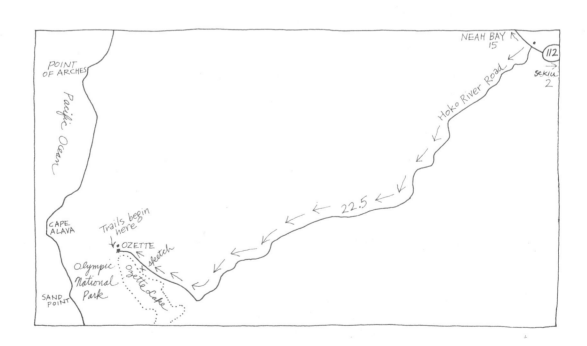

POINT OF ARCHES

Pacific Ocean

CAPE ALAVA

Trails begin here

OZETTE

Olympic National Park

Ozette Lake

SAND POINT

sketch

22.5

NEAH BAY 15

112

SEKIU 2

Hoko River Road

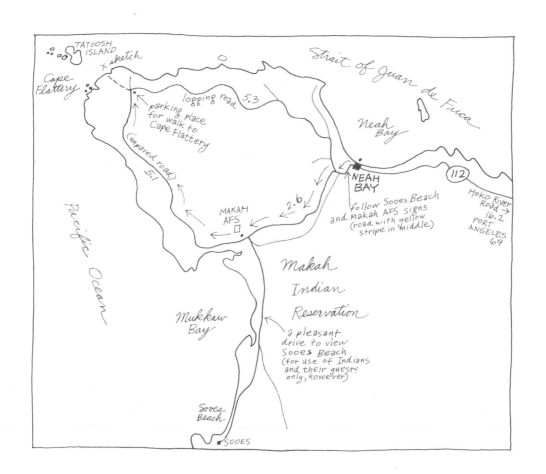

TATOOSH ISLAND

Cape Flattery

× sketch

Strait of Juan de Fuca

logging road   5.3

Neah Bay

parking place
for walk to
Cape Flattery

(unpaved road)   5.1

Pacific Ocean

MAKAH AFS

2.6

NEAH BAY

follow Sooes Beach
and Makah AFS signs
(road with yellow
stripe in middle)

112

Hoko River
Road →
16.2
PORT
ANGELES
69

Makah
Indian
Reservation

a pleasant
drive to view
Sooes Beach
(for use of Indians
and their guests
only, however)

Mukkaw Bay

Sooes Beach

SOOES

The road to Cape Flattery

It is foggy along the Strait of Juan de Fuca, so I am surprised and pleased to find Cape Flattery in bright sunshine. The trail to the dramatic viewpoint is a root-strewn path. The roots spread out from the base of ancient red cedars and sitka spruce. Scores of boats pass by, including a black-hulled sailing ship. A young bald eagle pursued by seabirds flies to cover in the forest. Feeling a part of all the drama, I sketch the island from a cliffside perch, as Tatoosh's lighthouse horn booms a mournful cry across the sunlit sea.

Tatoosh Island, Cape Flattery, Clallum County

The road to Obstruction Point

The road to Soleduck, the road along the Elwha River, and the road to Hurricane Ridge are beautiful trips and easily driven. The road to Obstruction Point, which takes off from Hurricane Ridge, is bumpy and steep at times. There are astonishing vistas to enjoy, including an expansive view of Puget Sound with snow-capped Mount Baker on the horizon.

Alpine flowers carpet the hillsides and sub-Alpine fir make spiky vignettes on the slopes where I sketch some of the glacier-carved peaks of Olympic National Park. Competitors in a footrace, which began at Deer Park, run past and greet me with a smile and wave of the hand.

Avalanche Lily, Clallum County

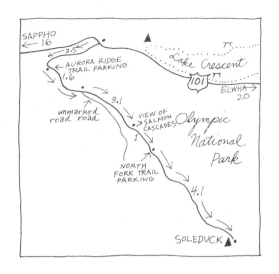

SAPPHO 16

Lake Crescent

101

ELWHA 2.0

2.5

AURORA RIDGE
TRAIL PARKING

1.6

unmarked
road road

3.1

VIEW OF
SALMON
CASCADES

1

Olympic
National
Park

NORTH
FORK TRAIL
PARKING

4.1

SOLEDUCK

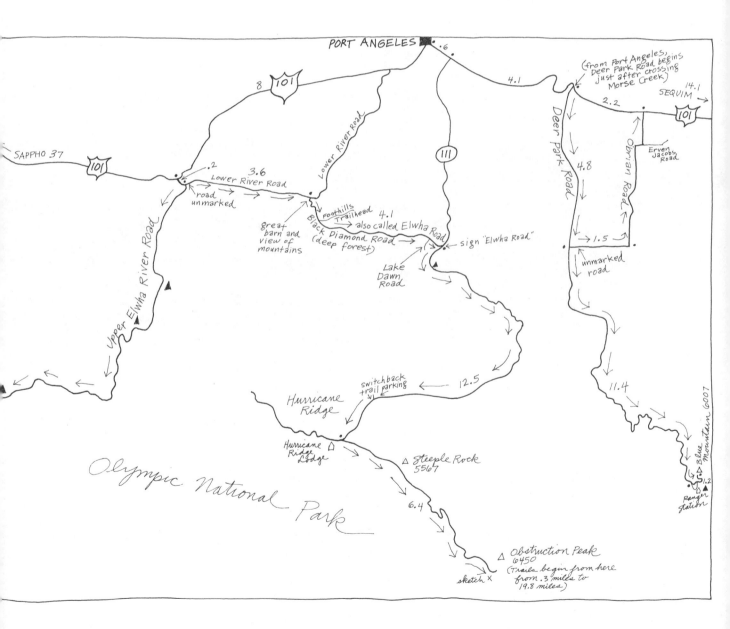

PORT ANGELES   .6

8   101

4.1

(from Port Angeles,
Deer Park Road begins
just after crossing
Morse Creek)

SEQUIM   14.1

2.2

101

SAPPHO 37

101

.2

Lower River Road

3.6

Lower River Road

111

Deer Park Road

O'brian Road

Erven
Jacobs
Road

4.8

road
unmarked

great
barn and
view of
mountains

Foothills
Trailhead

4.1
also called Elwha Road

Black Diamond Road
(deep forest)

sign "Elwha Road"

Lake
Dawn
Road

1.5

unmarked
road

Upper Elwha River Road

switchback
trail parking

Hurricane
Ridge

12.5

11.4

Hurricane
Ridge
Lodge

△ Steeple Rock
5567

Blue
Mountain 6007

1.2

Ranger
station

Olympic National Park

6.4

△ Obstruction Peak
6450
(Trails begin from here
from .3 miles to
19.8 miles)

sketch X

Mt. Olympus
from Obstruction Point,
Clallum County

63

Piper Bell,
found only in
Olympic
National Park

Bush
Cinquefoil,
Blue Mountain,
Olympic National
Park

Deer Park Road to Blue Mountain

The sharp, upthrust peaks of the Olympic Range are some 70 million years old but, geologically, they are considered new mountains. The serious exploration of the Olympics began in 1889 when James Christie, financed by a Seattle newspaper, led a trip into the mountains.

From time to time the passing of oncoming vehicles requires great caution on the narrow road toward the top of Blue Mountain. At the crest, on that pleasant clear day, I let time slip away and forget my own concerns, as I look out on the spaciousness of nature. In their rock crevice habitat I sketch buttery yellow cinquefoil and pale lavender piper bell, found only in Olympic National Park.

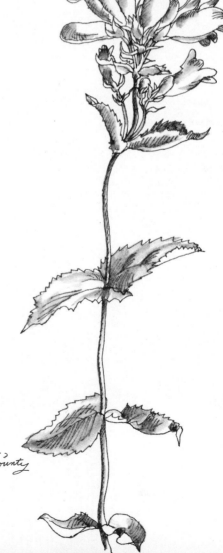

Lowbush
Penstemon,
Clallum County

The road from Port Gamble

Port Gamble, a historic mill town on a bluff overlooking the Hood Canal, was built by settlers to resemble their beloved East Machias, Maine. Saint Paul's Episcopal Church, 1870, was modeled after the Congregational Church of East Machias.

The steeple bell arrived by sailing vessel in 1879 and still calls people to worship on Sundays. I enjoy reading sentimental epitaphs in the shaded graveyard overlooking the canal.

One reads, "Shed not for her the bitter tear/Nor give the heart to vain regret/Tis but the casket that lies here/The gem that filled it sparkles yet."

St. Paul's Church, Port Gamble, Kitsap County

If you stay off Hwy. 20 and go
straight, the road comes out on 19th Street.
Go right on Walker Street and left on
Washington street.

follow Monroe,
Roosevelt and
Jackson sts.
to Fort

4.8

Cape
George

Fort
Worden State Park

unmarked
road

x sketch

PORT
TOWNSEND

Mystery
Bay

Admiralty Inlet

Beckett
point

20

2.8

Discovery Bay
to left

sketch
x

Fort
Flagler
State Park

Port Discovery Bay

1.1

.3

Indian
Island

2.9

County
Road 12

.3

1.9

IRONDALE

Marrowstone Island

County
Road 18

.8

NORDLAND

2.7

.4

Jefferson County Parke

East
Marrowstone
Road
Robbins Rd.

8.3

Puget Sound

PORT
LUDLOW

2.9

104

3

.4

104

Shine Rd.

Bywater
Bay Road

2.9

PORT GAMBLE

W.R. Hicks
County Parke

3

Hood Canal

Turnoff for Hood
Canal Ferry

x sketch

104

SOUTH
POINT

Ferry

3

4.5

104

68

a trip to Marrowstone Island

In 1792 Captain George Vancouver
of the Royal British Navy charted the
entrance to Puget Sound and found that
the high bluffs of the island there looked
as if they were composed of marrow stone.
(The island was named after this material.)
Fort Flagler State Park is situated on the
north end of the island and, while there, I
draw a view of the 1895 lighthouse, Puget
Sound, and Mount Baker. Many of the
original buildings of Fort Flagler, founded
in 1887, are still standing and are
part of the fascination of
Marrowstone Island.

Road to Port Townsend

There is a sign, hand-painted by the
ranger, at Rothschild House in Port
Townsend. It says, "111 YEARS OLD.
MOST ITEMS ORIGINAL. ENTRY WALL-
PAPER—1891, PARLOR—1885.
  YOUNGEST DAUGHTER LIVED HERE
78 YEARS, LAST 36 ALONE. MR. R.
  OWNED GEN. STORE DOWN TOWN.
5 CHILDREN, 3 GRAND. YOUNGEST SON
  GAVE HOUSE TO STATE PARKS
  IN 1958. A NICE FAMILY MEMORIAL!"
         Port Townsend was named
by Captain George Vancouver in 1792
  in honor of the Marquis
of Townshend. It has
many buildings and
  houses of historic
interest and is
picturesquely
situated on a
bluff overlooking
the bay and
Admiralty
Inlet.
  Fort Worden
State Park
nearby, with its
fort buildings
and old lighthouse,
is also quite
interesting.

Henry's
original
stove,
Rothschild
House,
Port
Townsend,
Jefferson
County

70

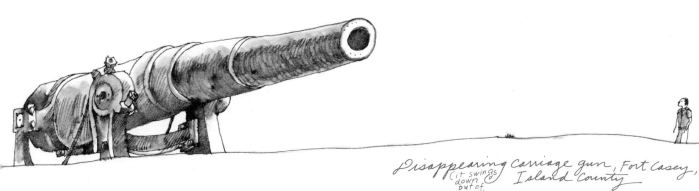

Disappearing carriage gun, Fort Casey, Island County
(it swings down out of sight)

Fort Casey to Coupeville and Oak Harbor

Big gun emplacements overlook Admiralty Inlet and point at passing ships. While I sketch, a work party of young people are painting the guns, which glisten in their new olive gray coat. The old lighthouse is now a display center, with photographs and historical material.

There are three state parks on Whidbey Island: Fort Casey, South Whidbey, and Deception Pass.

If you pick up an Island County map you may investigate all the roads on quiet, agricultural Whidbey Island.

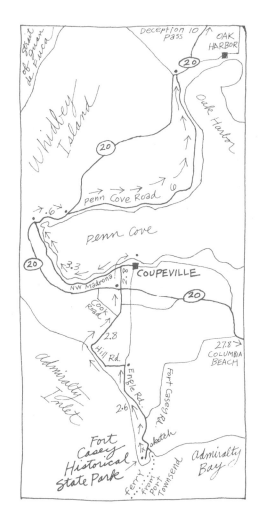

Strait of Juan de Fuca

Deception Pass 10

OAK HARBOR

Whidbey Island

20

Oak Harbor

20

Penn Cove Road   .6

.6

Penn Cove

20

3.3

NW Madrona

COUPEVILLE

20

Cook Road

2.8

Hill Rd.

Engle Rd.

Fort Casey Rd.

27.8 COLUMBIA BEACH

Admiralty Inlet

2.6

Fort Casey Historical State Park

sketch

Ferry from Port Townsend

Admiralty Bay

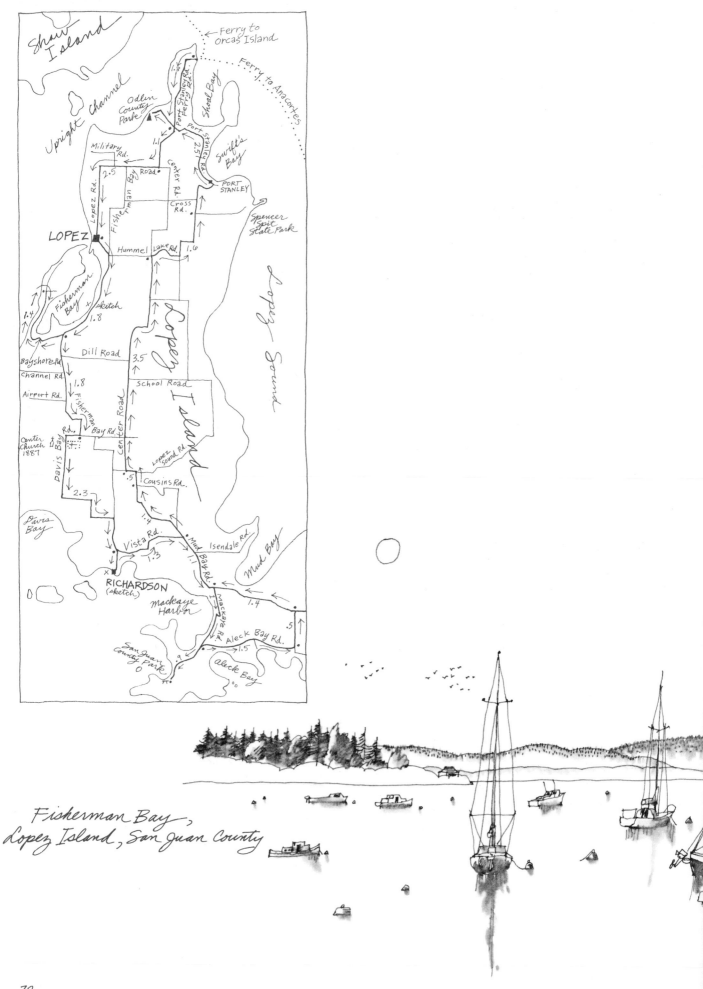

Shaw Island

Ferry to Orcas Island

Ferry to Anacortes

Upright Channel

Odlin County Park

Port Stanley Ferry Rd.

Shoal Bay

Military Rd.

2.5

Lopez Rd.

Center Rd.

Fisherman Bay Road

2.5

1.1

Swift's Bay

PORT STANLEY

LOPEZ

Cross Rd.

1.6

Hummel Lake Rd.

Spencer Spit State Park

Fisherman Bay

x sketch

1.4

1.8

Lopez Island

Lopez Sound

Dill Road

3.5

Bayshore Rd.

Channel Rd.

1.8

Airport Rd.

Fisherman Bay Rd.

School Road

Center Road

Lopez Sound Rd.

Center Church 1887

Davis Bay Rd.

2.3

.5

Cousins Rd.

1.4

Davis Bay

Vista Rd.

Isendale Rd.

Mud Bay

1.33

Mud Bay Rd.

1.1

RICHARDSON (sketch)

Mackaye Harbor

1.4

.5

Mackaye Rd.

Aleck Bay Rd.

San Juan County Park

.9

1.5

Aleck Bay

Fisherman Bay,
Lopez Island, San Juan County

72

Back road on Lopez Island —

   It is incredibly calm at Fisherman Bay in
the early morning. Motorboats have not started
up as yet and the cries of seabirds resound
across the water.

At Richardson I sketch the Richardson
General Store. A friendly place, its shelves
and tables are crowded with groceries, dry
goods, sundries, and hardware. The village
was settled by George Richardson, who
established a farm there about 1870.
A lively fishing port around 1900, it is
now again a quiet and serene village.

Richardson General Store,
Lopez Island, San Juan County

Orcas Island Road

On the way to Orcas Island the ferry stops at the charming, well-tended, flower-bedecked dock at Shaw Island. Nuns are arriving to open the little chapel on the pier. This island, although quite lovely, seems somewhat private, and I continue on to Orcas.

Orcas is the largest of the 172 islands that comprise the archipelago of the San Juans. I drive to the top of the 2,400-foot Mount Constitution for views of the islands and mainland beyond. A sign from the 1890s declares this to be "the finest marine view in all of North America." A stone tower at the top, built in the 1930s, was patterned after 12th-century European watchtowers.

Its architect had this message engraved in metal at the site: "To him who restores, my sincere commendation. To one who would alter, eternal damnation." Ellsworth Storey, 1936.

Orcas Island ferry,
San Juan County

President Channel

West Beach

West Beach Rd. .3

2.4 1.3

.5 EAST SOUND

East Sound

4.1

△ Mt. Constitution 2409

4.8

Mountain Lake

4.3

East Sound Road

1.4

Cascade Lake

1.4

Island

4

.9

ROSARIO RESORT

olga and Doebay Road

Doebay

Rosario Channel

DEER HARBOR

West Sound

Orcas

OLGA

2.6

ORCAS

Ferry to Friday Harbor

Ferry to Lopez

Shaw Island

77

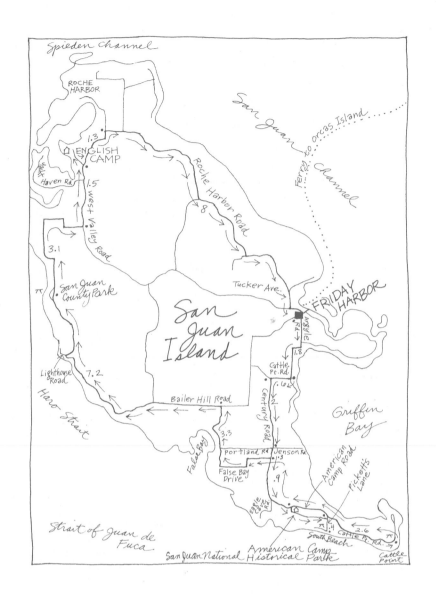

Spieden Channel

ROCHE HARBOR

San Juan to Orcas Island

Ferry to Orcas Island Channel

1.3

ENGLISH CAMP

Yacht Haven Rd.

1.5

West Valley Road

Roche Harbor Road

8

3.1

San Juan County Park

San Juan Island

Tucker Ave.

FRIDAY HARBOR

Argyle Rd.

1.8

Cattle Pt. Rd.

Lighthouse Road

7.2

2

Griffin Bay

Haro Strait

Bailer Hill Road

Century Road

3.3

False Bay

Portland Rd. Jenson Rd.

.3

False Bay Drive

.9

American Camp Road

Pickett's Lane

Eagle Cove Rd.

1.4

2.6 Cattle Pt. Rd.

South Beach

Cattle Point

Strait of Juan de Fuca

San Juan National Historical Park

American Camp

Fort English, San Juan Island,
San Juan County

Roads of San Juan

At the National Park on the road around the island there is a historical display. At South Beach the shore is long and strewn with water-worn logs. Farther on is a good view of False Bay with the Olympic mountain range in the background. With the tide out, there are plenty of tide pools to inspect.

At English Camp I sketch the blockhouse built around 1860 when the old fort was in its heyday. The British flag is still flown here, respecting the peaceful settlement of a border dispute in which they declared the San Juan Islands to be American rather than Canadian land. There is a grove of magnificent maple trees nearby, and the ranger tells me that one tree that has been core-tested is over three hundred years old.

Road to La Conner and Mount Vernon

Colorful flower baskets ornament stores along the main street of the fishing village of La Conner. I sketch the town from across the Swinomish Channel. Gaches Mansion, a twenty-two-room historic house on Second Street, is at top left in the picture, and a big blue-and-white sockeye salmon purse seiner boat is in the foreground.

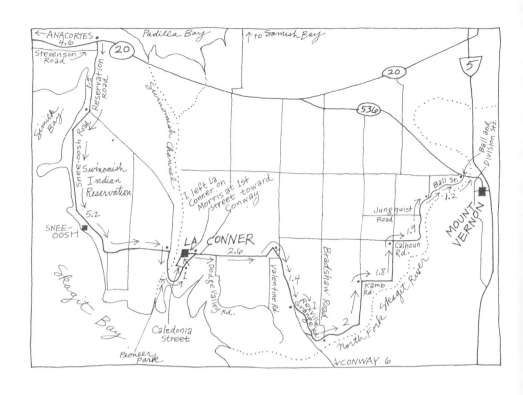

A Swinomish Indian boy, who watches me draw, tells me proudly that he has an eighteen-foot boat with which he fishes for king salmon. Just then a large pleasure boat passes with an auxiliary boat perched on it. "Lotsa cash for that," he says, "the boat on the stern is as big as mine."

The purse seiner is being readied for sea and, before I finish my drawing, its crew waves good-bye to relatives ashore as it sails away.

Sockeye Purse Seiner, La Conner, Skagit County

Samish Bay,
Skagit County

Samish Bay road

A steep wooden stairway goes to Samish Island Public Beach, which offers fifteen hundred feet of tideland for people's use. The bay is a spawning ground for the Pacific oyster, and intertidal hardshell clams and Dungeness crabs can be found at the beach at low tide.

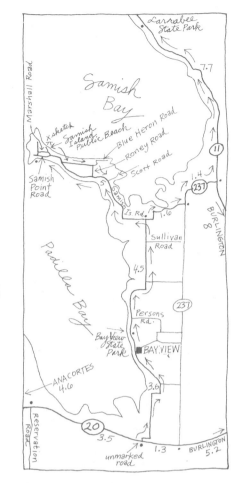

This beach of rocks and barnacles is a most tranquil place. There is the faint hum of commerce in the distance, but the cries of seabirds fill the air. A great blue heron flies by and I can hear the air rush through its wings.

McCORMICK-DEERING

The road to Lynden

The Peace Arch in Blaine commemorates the hundred years of open border shared by Canada and the United States between 1814 and 1914. After visiting the arch and its gardens, I drive through green, rolling meadowlands to Lynden. At Hans C. Berthusen Park, an ideal picnic spot, I draw the red barn shown on the next page with its bold white markings. Hans and Lida's old stump privy stands to the right of the barn. On the left is a 1906 threshing machine. Old tractors and antique farm machinery are arriving for Lynden's annual threshing bee and each engine makes its own "pock pock" sound. I sketch a McCormick-Deering W61 tractor from the thirties, nicknamed "The Outhouse" after its box like homemade cab.

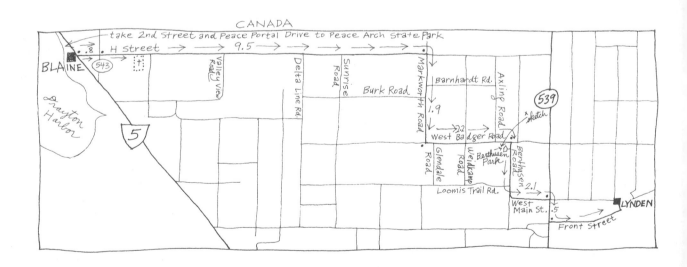

"The Outhouse",
Lynden, Whatcom County

Berthusen Barn, Lynden, Whatcom County

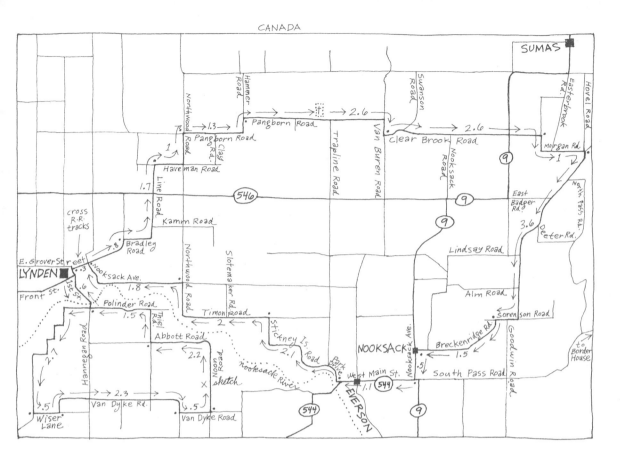

CANADA

SUMAS

Northwood Road
Hammer Road
1.3
1
Pangborn Road
Pangborn Road
2.6
Clay Rd.
Haveman Road
1.7
Line Road
546
Van Buren Road
Traeline Road
Swanson Road
Clear Brook Road
2.6
Easterbrook Rd.
Hovel Road
Morgan Rd.
1
9
Nooksack Road
9
East Badger Rd.
North Pass Rd.
3.6
Deter Rd.
cross
R.R.
tracks
Kamm Road
.8
Bradley
Road
Northwood Road
Slotemaker Rd.
Lindsay Road
E. Grover Street
LYNDEN
Nooksack Ave.
.3
1st St.
.6
1.8
Front St.
Polinder Road
1.5
Thiel Rd.
Timon Road
2
Stickney Is. Road
Park Dr.
Alm Road
Sorenson Road
Goodwin Road
to
Border
House
Hannegan Road
2.7
Abbott Road
2.2
Noon Road
2.1
Nooksack River
Breckenridge Rd.
1.5
.5
NOOKSACK
Nooksack Ave.
West Main St.
1.1
544
South Pass Road
.5
2.3
Van Dyke Rd.
.5
X sketch
EVERSON
.5
Wiser
Lane
Van Dyke Road
544
9

88

Roads around Lynden

The Dutch heritage of Lynden's settlers is reflected in the tidy character of its homes and farms. The neatness is enhanced by rows of flowers in gardens and window boxes. Big, handsome barns dot the green landscape. I sketch the graceful yellow-and-white Dykstra brothers' 1930s milking barn, which towers over the original barn. The new metal milking barn (not as picturesque) is to the left, out of my picture.

The Dykstra brothers' Barn,
Whatcom County

The road to Border House

This route touches the Canadian border, although no legal road continues from here into Canada. The proprietor of Border House has many a whimsical display for the enjoyment of visitors. The wagon and milk cans in my drawing are painted red, white, and blue. All the birds pictured are alive except the owl. A tour of the quaint, Greek Revival-style house includes a peek at the Teddy Roosevelt room, where he is supposed to have spent the night.

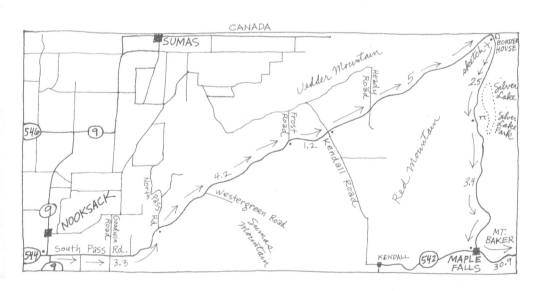

Sign at Border House, Whatcom County

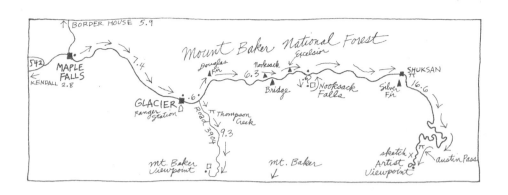

Mount Baker National Forest

BORDER HOUSE 5.9

542 MAPLE FALLS

KENDALL 2.8

7.4

GLACIER
Ranger Station

Road 39.04

Thompson Creek
9.3

mt. Baker Viewpoint

Douglas Fir

6.3 Nooksack

Bridge

Nooksack Falls

Excelsior

mt. Baker

SHUKSAN

16.6

Silver Fir

sketch
Artist
Viewpoint

austin Pass

92

The road to Mount Baker

A wet gravel road banked with snow leads to Artist Point, which is supposed to provide a good view of Mount Baker. Once there, I am enveloped in thick, misty clouds and only occasionally does a break appear in the rolling fogbanks. I decide not to go away empty-handed, however, so here you see a drawing of the foreground. You must drive to Artist Point to put mighty Mount Baker in the background and complete my picture!

Timber line,
Mt. Baker,
Whatcom County

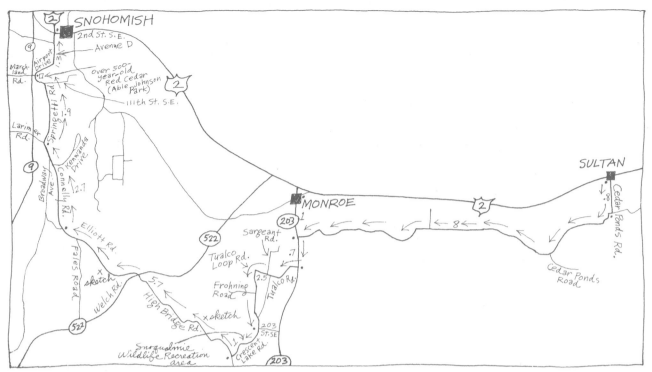

Map labels

SNOHOMISH

2nd St. S.E.
Avenue D

Airport Drive

1.3

over 500-
year-old
Red Cedar
(Able Johnson
Park)

111th St. S.E.

2

March-
land
Rd.

9

Larimer
Rd.

Springetti Rd.

1.9

Kenwanda
Drive

2.7

Connelly Rd.

9

Broadway Ave.

Elliott Rd.

522

Fales Road

× sketch

Welch Rd.

5.7

High Bridge Rd.

× sketch

522

Snoqualmie
Wildlife Recreation
area

.1

Crescent
Lake Rd.

203
St. SE

203

MONROE

203

1

Sargeant
Rd.

Tualco
Loop Rd.

Frohning
Road

2.5

Tualco Rd.

.7

8

2

SULTAN

Cedar Ponds Rd.

.8

Cedar Ponds
Road

Back road from Sultan to Snohomish

The road from Sultan follows the
Skykomish River. From Tualco Road the
scenery is green and hilly with
dairy-country barns and
farmhouses silhouetted against
forest backgrounds. Along the
way I sketch a small milking
barn that has been fashioned into
a house. At Ricville farm I
draw a landscape encompassing
most of the farm's buildings
and some of the Holstein herd.

milking barn-house,
near Monroe,
Snohomish County

94

Snohomish County farm

Tom Thumb Grocery,
Granite Falls,
Snohomish County

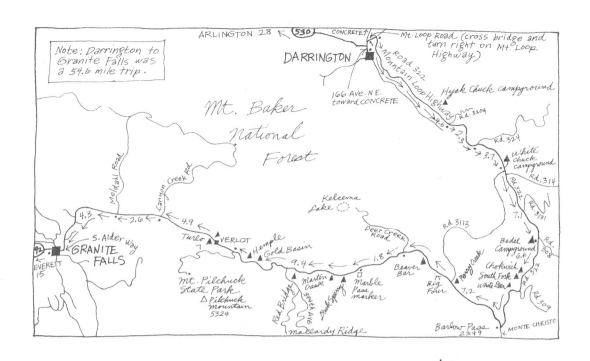

Note: Darrington to Granite Falls was a 54.6 mile trip.

ARLINGTON 28 ← 530 CONCRETE↑

DARRINGTON

Mt. Loop Road (cross bridge and turn right on Mt. Loop Highway)

166 Ave. N.E. toward CONCRETE

Road 322 Mountain Loop Highway

Hyak Chuck campground

Rd. 3204

4.6 • 2.3

Rd. 324

3.7

White chuck campground

Rd. 314

Mt. Baker National Forest

Kelcema Lake

Deer Creek Road

Rd. 3113

Rd. 322

7.1

Rd. 3131

Bedal Campground 6.6

Rd. 308

Chokwich South Fork White Bear

Rd. 322

Rd. 309

Meldahi Road

Canyon Creek Rd.

4.3 ← 2.6 • ← 4.9

Turlo ▲ VERLOT

Hemple Gold Basin

9.4 ←

1.8

Beaver Bar

Perry Creek

7.2

92 EVERETT 15

GRANITE FALLS

S. Alder Way

Mt. Pilchuck State Park △ Pilchuck Mountain 5324

Red Bridge

South Ave.

Marten Creek

Bush Quarry

Marble Pass marker

Big Four

Barlow Pass 2349

↓ MONTE CHRISTO

Mackardy Ridge

Road to Granite Falls

From the lumber town of Darrington, this back road wanders through Mount Baker National Forest. Hemlock, big-leaf maple, vine maple, and alder flourish here. The trunks of the older white alder trees are spotted with green moss. When growing in profusion, they create incredibly intricate patterns in the forest. At Granite Falls I enjoy visiting the busy Tom Thumb Grocery and sketching its aging facade.

Self Heal (purple flowers), Snohomish County

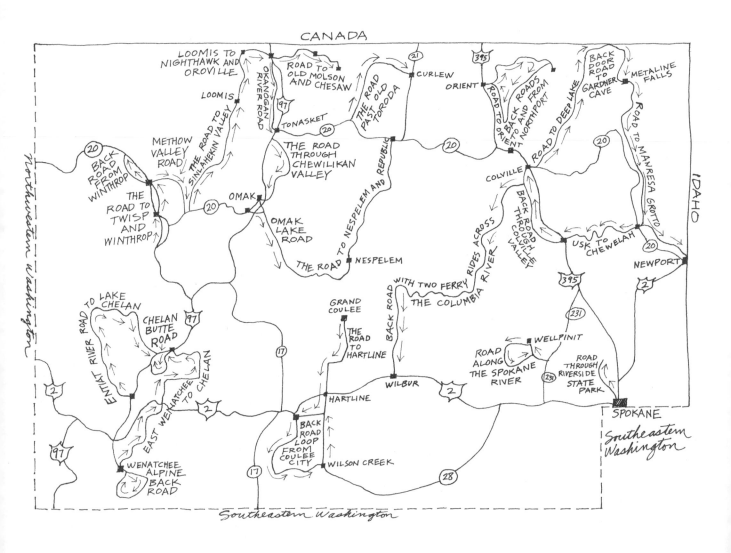

CANADA

LOOMIS TO
NIGHTHAWK AND
OROVILLE

LOOMIS

ROAD TO
OLD MOLSON
AND CHESAW

(21)

CURLEW

ORIENT

(395)

BACK
DOOR
ROAD
TO
GARDNER
CAVE

METALINE
FALLS

OKANOGAN RIVER ROAD

THE ROAD PAST OLD TORODA

TONASKET

(97)

(20)

THE ROAD TO SINLAHEKIN VALLEY

METHOW
VALLEY
ROAD

THE ROAD
THROUGH
CHEWILIKAN
VALLEY

ROAD TO ORIENT

BACK ROADS TO AND FROM NORTHPORT

ROAD TO DEEP LAKE

ROAD TO MANRESA GROTTO

(20)

(20)

(20)

BACK
ROAD
FROM
WINTHROP

OMAK

COLVILLE

(20)

THE
ROAD TO
TWISP
AND
WINTHROP

(20)

OMAK
LAKE
ROAD

THE ROAD TO NESPELEM AND REPUBLIC

BACK ROAD THROUGH COLVILLE VALLEY

USK TO CHEWELAH

NEWPORT

(2)

THE ROAD

NESPELEM

BACK ROAD WITH TWO FERRY RIDES ACROSS THE COLUMBIA RIVER

ROAD TO LAKE CHELAN

ENTIAT RIVER

CHELAN
BUTTE
ROAD

(97)

GRAND
COULEE

(395)

WELLPINIT

THE
ROAD
TO
HARTLINE

ROAD
ALONG
THE
SPOKANE
RIVER

ROAD
THROUGH
RIVERSIDE
STATE
PARK

(231)

(2)

(2)

(17)

(231)

EAST WENATCHEE TO CHELAN

(2)

WILBUR

(2)

SPOKANE

Southeastern
Washington

(97)

WENATCHEE
ALPINE
BACK
ROAD

(17)

HARTLINE

BACK
ROAD
LOOP
FROM
COULEE
CITY

WILSON CREEK

(28)

Southeastern Washington

Northeastern Washington

IDAHO

100

Northeastern Washington

I remember the broad glacially formed valleys and their majestic rivers, the Methow, Okanogan, Similkameen, Kettle, Sanpoil, Pend Oreille, the great Columbia, and others.

I recall orchards bulging with apples; the deep forests of pine, fir, and larch; the lakes of silver hue; and vast wheat fields awaiting harvest, all this along the intriguing back roads of northeastern Washington.

Pearly Everlasting
(white flowers)
Chelan County

Washington apples,
Chelan County

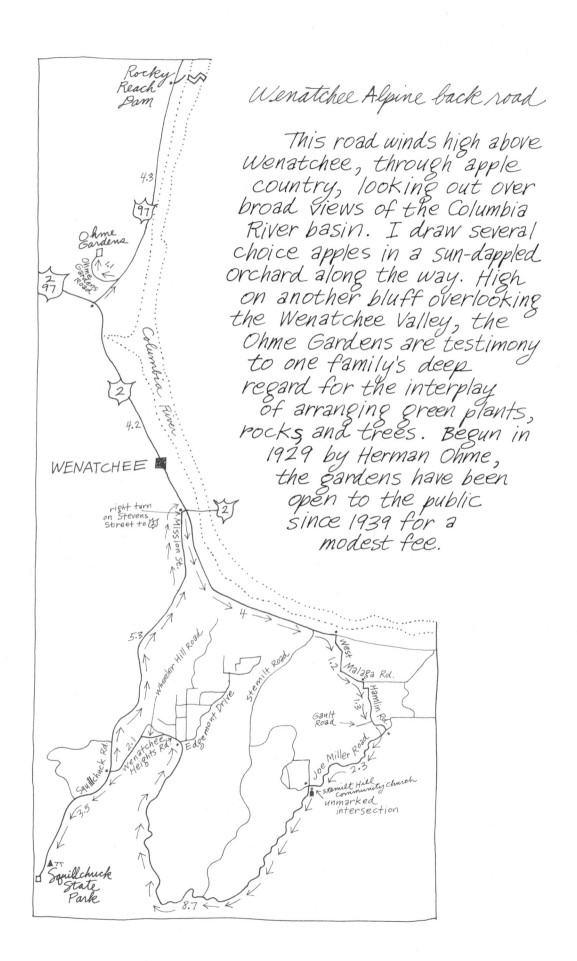

Wenatchee Alpine back road

This road winds high above Wenatchee, through apple country, looking out over broad views of the Columbia River basin. I draw several choice apples in a sun-dappled orchard along the way. High on another bluff overlooking the Wenatchee Valley, the Ohme Gardens are testimony to one family's deep regard for the interplay of arranging green plants, rocks, and trees. Begun in 1929 by Herman Ohme, the gardens have been open to the public since 1939 for a modest fee.

Rocky Reach Dam

4.3

97

Ohme Gardens

7 97

Ohme Gardens Road

Columbia River

2

4.2

WENATCHEE

right turn on Stevens Street to 2

Mission St.

2

5.3

Wheeler Hill Road

4

West Malaga Rd.

1.2

Stemilt Road

Hamlin Rd.

1.3

Gault Road

Edgemont Drive

2.1

Wenatchee Heights Rd.

Squilchuck Rd.

Joe Miller Road

2.3

3.5

Stemilt Hill Community Church
unmarked intersection

Squilchuck State Park

8.7

Log interior,
St. Andrews Church,
Chelan, Chelan County

104

East Wenatchee to Chelan

There are expansive views along this road of Wenatchee and the Columbia River. Ahead are the purple-hued bluffs of Badger Mountain. Once you have gone over the mountain and through McGinnis Canyon, the road affords a dramatic view of the farming area around Waterville.

The sky darkens in the distance as rain threatens, yet the wheat fields are drenched in the afternoon sun.

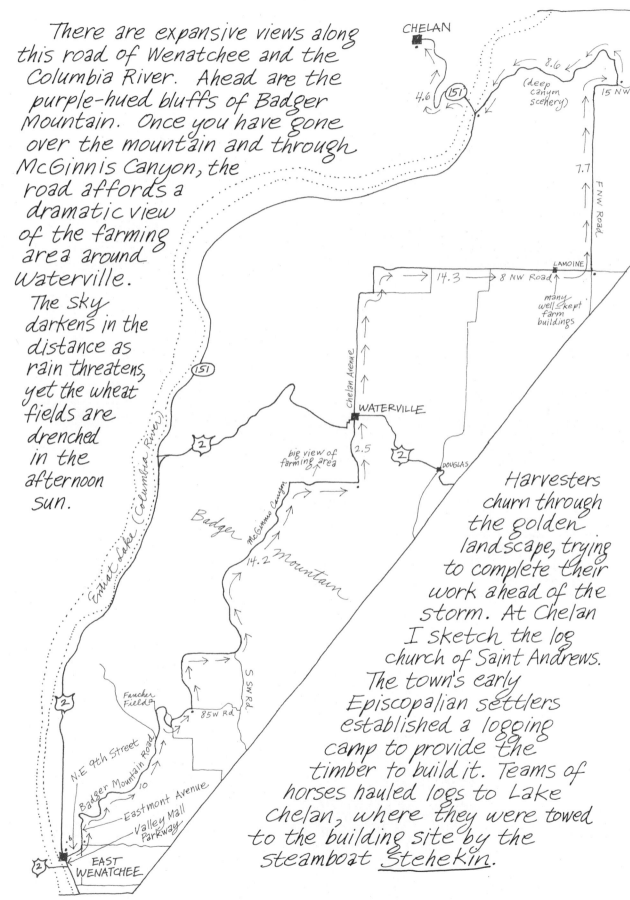

CHELAN

4.6 151 8.6

(deep canyon scenery)

15 NW Rd.

7.7 F NW Road

LAMOINE

14.3 8 NW Road

many well-kept farm buildings

Chelan Avenue

WATERVILLE

2.5

2 **DOUGLAS**

151

2

big view of farming area

Badger McGinnis Canyon

14.2 Mountain

S SW Rd.

Fancher Field

85 W Rd.

2

N.E 9th Street

Badger Mountain Road

10

Eastmont Avenue

Valley Mall Parkway

Entiat Lake (Columbia River)

2 **EAST WENATCHEE**

Harvesters churn through the golden landscape, trying to complete their work ahead of the storm. At Chelan I sketch the log church of Saint Andrews. The town's early Episcopalian settlers established a logging camp to provide the timber to build it. Teams of horses hauled logs to Lake Chelan, where they were towed to the building site by the steamboat <u>Stehekin</u>.

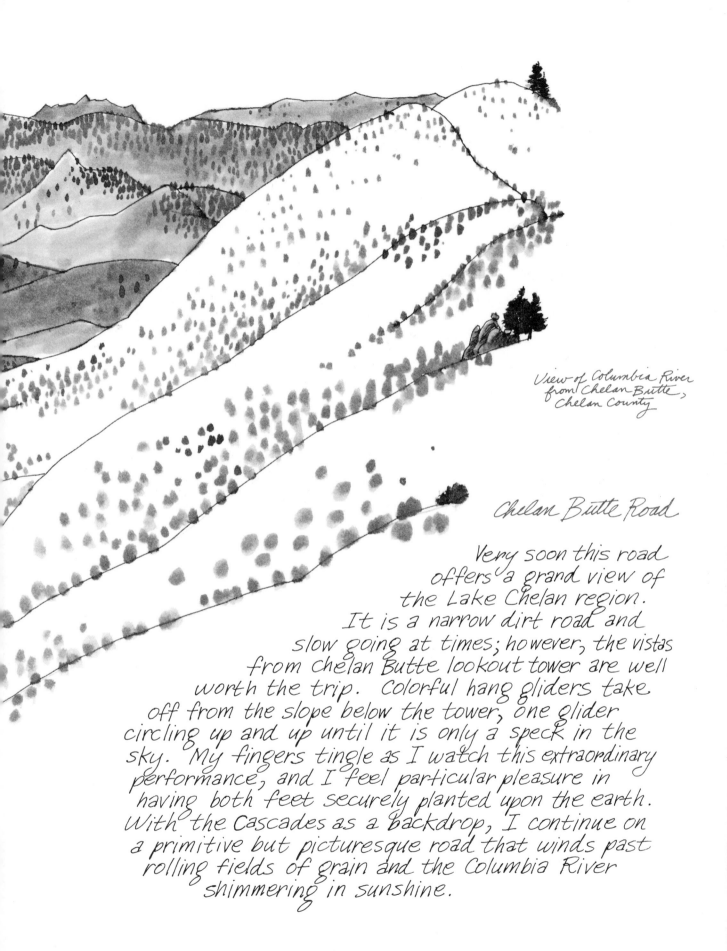

View of Columbia River
from Chelan Butte,
Chelan County

Chelan Butte Road

Very soon this road
offers a grand view of
the Lake Chelan region.
It is a narrow dirt road and
slow going at times; however, the vistas
from Chelan Butte lookout tower are well
worth the trip. Colorful hang gliders take
off from the slope below the tower, one glider
circling up and up until it is only a speck in the
sky. My fingers tingle as I watch this extraordinary
performance, and I feel particular pleasure in
having both feet securely planted upon the earth.
With the Cascades as a backdrop, I continue on
a primitive but picturesque road that winds past
rolling fields of grain and the Columbia River
shimmering in sunshine.

Entiat River Road to Chelan

Peach, pear, and apple orchards decorate the banks a good way along the Entiat River, then pine forest and more rustic mountain scenery take over. At the 6,600-foot elevation there is a viewpoint of great mountains with snow-topped Glacier Peak looming highest. The descent then begins to Lake Chelan, a road lined with wild flowers such as tansy, fireweed, Indian paintbrush, lupine, stonecrop, and yarrow.

Chelan County
apple orchard

Old Witte Homestead
near Winthrop,
Okanogan County

The road to Twisp
and Winthrop

    I follow the Methow
River for some miles,
paralleling highways 153
and 20. Between Twisp
and Winthrop I sketch
the old Witte Homestead,
the Methow placidly flowing
past its back door. A broad
field of green alfalfa is in
the foreground and the
mountains of the Okanogan
National Forest grace the skyline.

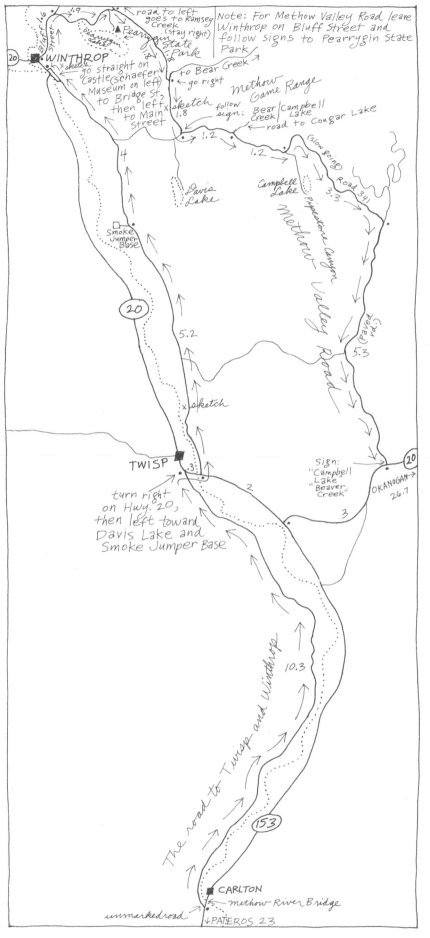

road to left
goes to Ramsey
Creek
(stay right)

Note: For Methow Valley Road leave
Winthrop on Bluff Street and
follow signs to Pearrygin State
Park

1.9
1.6
Bluff Street
Pearrygin State Park
▲ Pearrygin

20 ■ WINTHROP
x sketch

go straight on
Castle (Schaefer
Museum on left)
to Bridge St,
then left
to Main
Street

to Bear Creek →
← go right

x sketch
1.8
follow
sign: Bear | Campbell
Creek | Lake
← road to Cougar Lake

Methow
Game Range

1.2

Davis
Lake

Campbell
Lake

1.2 (slow going) Road 341

4

Methow Valley Road

Pipestone Canyon

3.3

Campbell
Lake

Smoke
Jumper
Base

20

5.2

(Paved rd.)
5.3

x sketch

Sign:
"Campbell
Lake
Beaver
Creek"

20

■ TWISP
.3

OKANOGAN →
26.7

turn right
on Hwy. 20,
then left toward
Davis Lake and
Smoke Jumper Base

2

3

The road to Twisp and Winthrop

10.3

153

■ CARLTON
← Methow River Bridge

unmarked road
↓ PATEROS 23

R-1 Box 241
THE
SLAG
WORKS
STROMBERGES

Seen along the
road to Winthrop,
Okanogan County

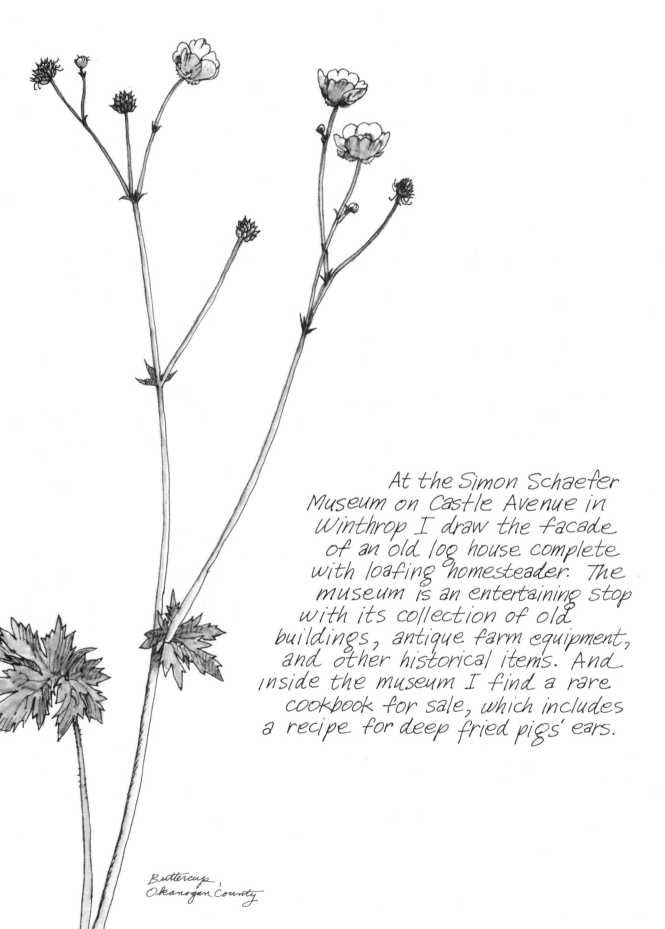

At the Simon Schaefer
Museum on Castle Avenue in
Winthrop I draw the facade
of an old log house complete
with loafing homesteader. The
museum is an entertaining stop
with its collection of old
buildings, antique farm equipment,
and other historical items. And
inside the museum I find a rare
cookbook for sale, which includes
a recipe for deep fried pigs' ears.

Buttercup,
Okanogan County

Old homesteader's cabin, Winthrop, Okanogan County

Back road
from
Winthrop

Goat Creek Road

sketch

X

20

Methow River

8.5

8.9

Chewack River

WINTHROP

cross bridge, follow sign to Sun Mt. and Fish Hatchery

FISH HATCHERY

.8   .5

.4

Twin Lakes Road

White Ave.

20

Back road from Winthrop

The road follows the Methow River through farming land and into primitive pine forest. Emerging from the thick forest I am back in farm country again. Sprinklers spray water all around, making green alfalfa crops still greener. Along the road I draw a chocolate-colored barn filled with golden-hued hay.

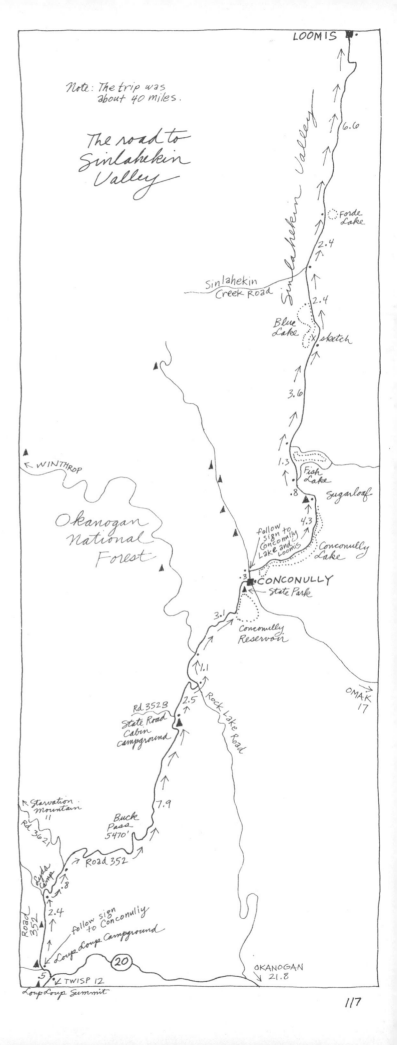

Note: The trip was about 40 miles.

The road to Sinlahekin Valley

LOOMIS

6.6

Sinlahekin Valley

Forde Lake

2.4

Sinlahekin Creek Road

2.4

Blue Lake

X sketch

3.6

1.3

Fish Lake

.8

Sugarloaf

follow sign to Conconully Lake and Loomis

4.3

Conconully Lake

.3

CONCONULLY

State Park

Okanogan National Forest

WINTHROP

3.1

Conconully Reservoir

1.1

OMAK 17

Rd 352 B

2.5

Rock Lake Road

State Road Cabin campground

7.9

Starvation Mountain 11

Rd 362.1

Buck Pass 5470'

Road 352

Lyda Camp

.8

Road 352

2.4

follow sign to Conconully

Loup Loup Campground

20

OKANOGAN 21.8

.5

TWISP 12

Loup Loup Summit

117

Methow Valley road
(map, page 112)
There are pleasing views of mountains and valleys along this road. I try to show this in my drawing and to move the eye forward and back again with overlapping ranges of hills, farmland, forest, and mountain peaks.

View of Methow Valley
near Winthrop, Okanogan County

The road to Sinlahekin Valley (map, page 117)

A good gravel road leads me through thick fir and pine forest to an old mining town once known as Salmon City. The more poetic name for this locale—Conconully—has survived. Translated from the Indian, it means "the beautiful land of the bunch grass flats."

Blue Lake south of Loomis,
Okanogan County

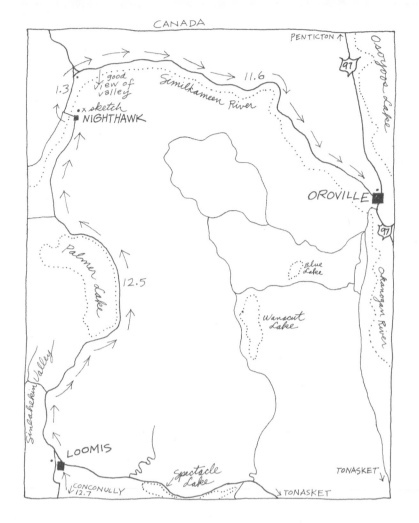

CANADA

PENTICTON ↑

97

Osoyoos Lake

good
view of
valley

Similkameen River

11.6

1.3

x sketch

■ NIGHTHAWK

OROVILLE ■

97

Palmer Lake

12.5

Blue
Lake

Okanogan River

Similkameen Valley

Wanacut
Lake

■ LOOMIS

↓ CONCONULLY
12.7

Spectacle
Lake

TONASKET

TONASKET

The Pink House, Nighthawk,
Okanogan County

Loomis to Nighthawk and Oroville

Rock-faced mountains, dotted with pines and firs, abruptly rise in a colorful blend of blue, gray, purple, and ocher from Sinlahekin Valley north of Loomis. Apple orchards grow at one end of Palmer Lake, while green grass carpets the southern end of the valley.

At the almost deserted mining town of Nighthawk I sketch the Pink House. It had once been a lively hostelry and perhaps even a place of questionable repute, I was told by local folks. The old store and post office and the former hotel are still there and occupied. Discoveries of precious metal in the early 1890s made both Loomis and Nighthawk booming mining towns. The boom ended in a few years, but the scenic beauty of the valley remains.

The road to Oroville follows the Similkameen River, where gold was panned in 1857.

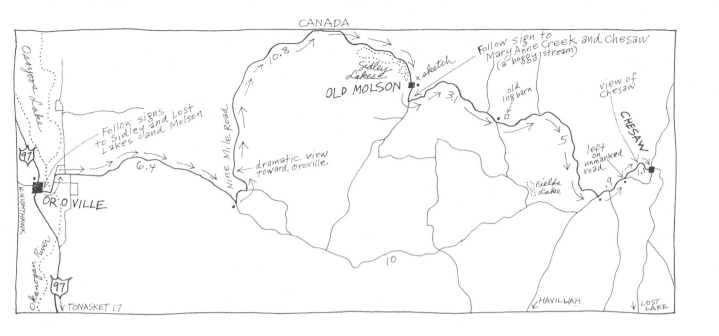

Road to Old Molson and Chesaw

The road parallels the Canadian border for almost a mile and later passes Sidley Lakes before entering Old Molson. Originally the town had a doctor, veterinarian, attorney, and a milliner; a drugstore, meat market, creamery, restaurant, furniture store, grocery store, harness shop, newspaper, and garage. When Kohrdt's Garage closed its doors for the last time in 1941, that was the end of Old Molson—except, of course, for the collection of early buildings, equipment, and memorabilia that remains there today.

Chesaw, too, has some of the same flavor. This town, once center of a mining district of over five hundred, claims it is named in honor of a Chinese miner named Joe Chee Saw.

OKANOGAN COUNTY HISTORICAL SOCIETY

OLD MOLSON

WELCOME FOLKS TO OLD MOLSON FOUNDED IN 1900. SHE WAS A LIVELY MINING CAMP UNTIL A FARMER CLAIMED THE WHOLE TOWN WAS PART OF HIS HOMESTEAD. WHILE THE DISPUTE RAGED, DISGUSTED CITIZENS FOUNDED NEW MOLSON HALF-A-MILE NORTH. PEOPLE, BUSINESSES, THE POST OFFICE - EVERYTHING MOVED TO NEW MOLSON. ITS RAILROAD STATION ELEV 3706 WAS THE HIGHEST IN THE STATE. THE ORIGINAL MOLSON FADED AWAY, BUT ITS MEMORIES LINGER IN THESE WEATHER-WORN BUILDINGS.

NO DOUBLE PARKING 3 HOUR PARKING LIMIT

DEPENDABLE CHAMPION SPARK PLUG SERVICE

THE STANDARD ZEROLENE FOR MOTOR CARS

AVOID PENALTY REPORT TO CUSTOMS VEHICLES ENTERING

Old Molson, Okanogan County

125

Okanogan River road

Countless apple trees, branches laden with red and yellow fruit, a forest of wooden poles supporting them, adorn the green banks of the Okanogan River. There are also grassy meadows, river views, farms, and sparsely wooded bluffs along the way to Tonasket.

Okanogan River Valley,
Okanogan County

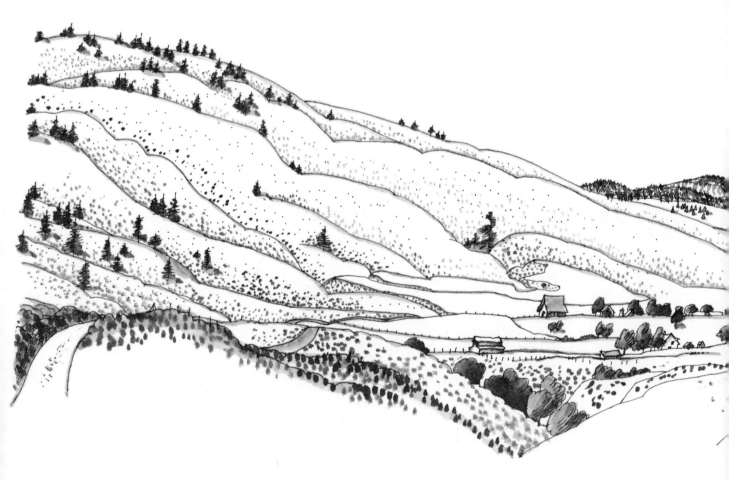

The road through Chewilikan Valley

Driving through rocky, sparse pine, and sagebrush country, I delight in the spectacular view of the Okanogan River winding its way through McLaughlin Canyon. On July 29, 1858, 149 miners led by James McLaughlin were ambushed by Indians in the canyon. One miner, Francis Wolff by name, could not control his horse. It galloped off without him in the direction of the ambushing Indians. He had packed $2,000 in gold dust on the creature and was determined not to lose it, so with great danger to himself, he managed to get the horse back in time (from the records of the Museum of Okanogan Historical Society). I sketch this grand view of quiet Chewilikan Valley. It has its own special beauty, with gray green sagebrush dotting the hills, golden grain crops in the valley, and distant dark green forest.

Chewilikan Valley,
Okanogan County

Lupine,
Okanogan County

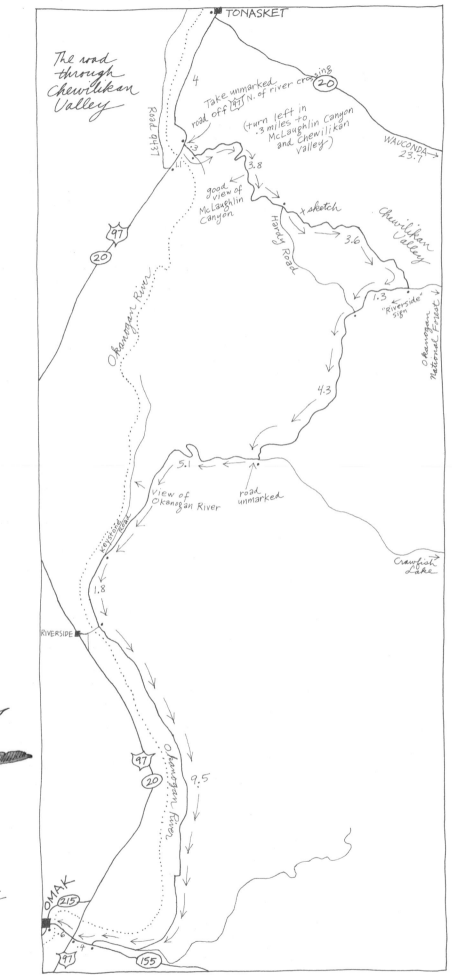

TONASKET

The road
through
Chewilikan
Valley

4

Take unmarked
road off 97 N. of river crossing

20

WAUCONDA→
23.7

(turn left in
.3 miles to
McLaughlin Canyon
and Chewilikan
Valley)

Road 9437

.3

1.1

3.8

good
view of
McLaughlin
Canyon

Hardy Road

+ sketch

3.6

Chewilikan Valley

97
20

Okanogan River

1.3

"Riverside"
Sign

Okanogan National Forest

4.3

5.1

View of
Okanogan River

road
unmarked

Crawfish
Lake

Keystone Road

1.8

RIVERSIDE

97
20

Okanogan River

9.5

OMAK
215

97
.4
.6

155

Balanced Rock,
Kartar Valley,
Okanogan County

Omak Lake Road

Attesting to Okanogan
County's great geological
variety, here at Omak Lake massive
rock formations jut majestically upward
from the blue green water. Along Kartar
Valley Road I sketch Balanced Rock
to the buzzing of bees and grasshoppers.
At Goose Lake there are plenty of
ducks among the bulrushes, and on
the road cows plump themselves
down and have to be nudged
up and along.

Omak Lake,
Okanogan County

The road to Nespelem and Republic

There is a dramatic view of the Columbia River along this back road to Nespelem. Once in town I visit the grave of Chief Joseph, the famous war leader of the Nez Percé Indians in the 1870s. He led his people fifteen hundred miles through Montana wilderness toward Canada, but was captured at the border by the United States Army. Finally sent to Colville Reservation, he ended his days in 1904 at Nespelem. Lettered on his gravestone is his Indian name, HIN-MAH-TOO-YAH-LAT-KEHT, "Thunder rolling in the mountains."

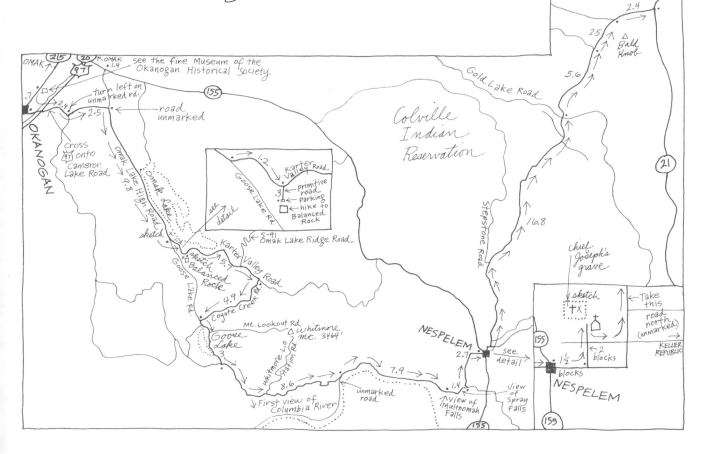

← WAUCONDA 17
30
REPUBLIC
30
21
Indian Museum near courthouse
14.7
Ten Mile Camp
2.4
2.5
Bald Knob
5.6
21

OMAK
215
20 → OMAK 1.4
97
see the fine Museum of the Okanogan Historical Society
Gold Lake Road
.7
2.4
2.5
turn left on unmarked rd.
road unmarked
155
Colville Indian Reservation
cross 97 onto Cameron Lake Road
Omak Lake High Road 9.8
Omak Lake
1.2
Karter Valley Road
.3 primitive road parking
hike to Balanced Rock
see detail
sketch
Karter Valley Road
5.1
sketch Balanced Rock
Goose Lake Rd.
S-91 Omak Lake Ridge Road
Goose Lake Rd
4.9
Coyote Creek Rd.
Mt. Lookout Rd
Whitmore Mt. 3464'
Goose Lake 1.0
Whitmore L.O. Station Rd.
Stepstone Road
16.8
8.6
First view of Columbia River
7.9
unmarked road
View of Multnomah Falls
NESPELEM
2.7
1.4
View of Spray Falls
see detail
Chief Joseph's grave
sketch +x
← Take this road north (unmarked)
155
1½ blocks
2 blocks
KELLER REPUBLIC
NESPELEM
155
155

134

HIN-MAH-TOO-
YAH-LAT-KEKT

THUNDER ROLLING IN
THE MOUNTAINS

CHIEF JOSEPH

Headstone
at Nespelem,
Okanogan County

135

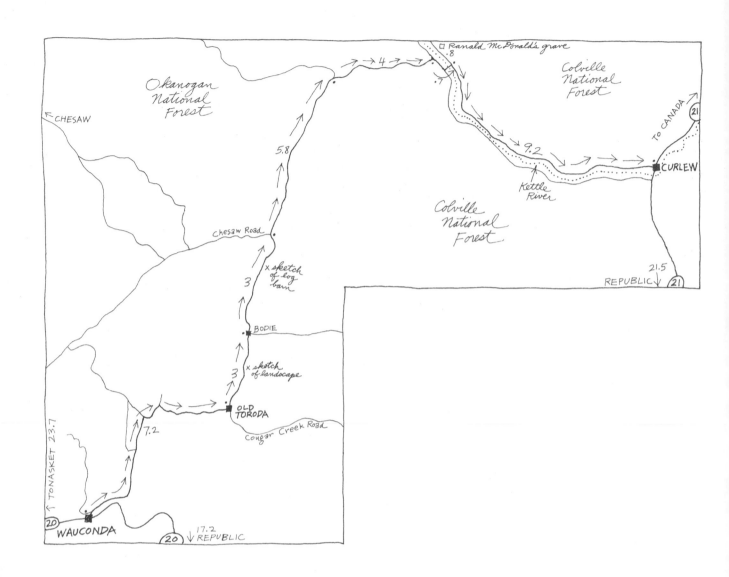

Okanogan
National
Forest

← CHESAW

5.8

Chesaw Road

x sketch
of log
barn

3

■ BODIE

3

x sketch
of landscape

■ OLD
TORODA

7.2

Cougar Creek Road

↑ TONASKET 23.7

⑳
WAUCONDA

⑳

↓ 17.2
REPUBLIC

→ → 4 →

□ Ranald McDonald's grave
.8

Colville
National
Forest

TO CANADA ↗ ㉑

9.2

Kettle
River

CURLEW

Colville
National
Forest

21.5
REPUBLIC ↓ ㉑

136

The road past Old Toroda

There are log homesteads at Old Toroda and a ghost town at Bodie. I sketch a swayback log house along the road, then discover a big log barn to draw at Single Shot Ranch a few miles past Bodie. Log barns and farmhouses give a quaint early American look to this narrow agricultural valley. Later, in Ferry County, during a very pretty drive along the Kettle River, I witness fly-fishermen trying their luck in the free-flowing stream. This brings me, finally, to the hamlet of Curlew.

Farm near Old Toroda,
Okanogan County

Log barn north of Bodie, Okanogan County

Back roads to and from Northport

From Orient, a back road goes past Little Pierre and Pierre Lakes. A fisherman at Pierre tells me he has fished cutthroat trout there since the 1930s. As he speaks, a great blue heron flies by chased by a hawk. Releasing plaintive cries all the while, the heron makes great maneuvers to escape the hawk. The road continues through thick forest, emerging eventually at Northport.

From Northport the scenery changes to views of the Columbia River and inland farms and woods. At Snag Cove I sketch the vast Franklin D. Roosevelt Lake portion of the Columbia River. Stalks of woolly mullein decorate the foreground of the picture.

Snag Cove,
Franklin D. Roosevelt Lake,
(Columbia River), Stevens County

141

Back road to and
from Northport

Sheep
Creek

25

Sheep
Creek
Rd.

American Fork
Limestone
Road

3

Elbow
Lake

12.6

Flagstaff
Lookout
Road

Limestone
Rd.

6.6

go right toward Sheep Creek
and Elbow Lake

Kiel Ridge
Road

Kiel Ridge Rd.

stay on road
to Elbow Lake
and Northport

unmarked
road

NORTHPORT

.8

395

cross river,
turn right

Pierre Lake

Fisher Creek Road

Flat Creek Road

Crown Creek Rd.

25

ORIENT

4.7

Little Pierre Lake

First Thought
Lookout Road

Mineral Mountain Road

9.9

2.3

Back road
to Orient

Kettle River

Pierre Lake Road

5

12.2

395

4

Kettle River Rd.

Snag Cove
Campground

(Columbia River)

sketch) X

.3.8

6.1

Flat Creek Rd.

Franklin D. Roosevelt Lake

25

395

KETTLE
FALLS

20

35
M.P.H.

Road to Orient

This back road runs through farming and forest land, affording many views of the winding Kettle River. The Orient weather station in my drawing is across the street from the grocery store. Two store owners I speak to confess that the humor of this sign helped them decide that Orient would be a good town to live in.

Weather station, Orient, Ferry County

ORIENT WEATHER STATION

OBSERVE ROCK:
If it is SWINGING,
  WIND is BLOWING.
If it is WHITE,
  It is SNOWING.
If it is WET,
  It is RAINING
If YOU CAN'T SEE ROCK
  It is FOGGY

144

The road past Deep Lake

Attractive meadows, old homesteads, and forest scenery are found on this trip north of Colville. Deep Lake, bathed in early morning mist, conveys a mood of serenity, calm, and mystery.

Several miles farther north of Deep Lake, I sketch the 1804 Johnson homestead with its laundry spread along the fence. People settled in this valley along Deep Creek at that time to work in the local lead mines.

The old Johnson homestead,
Leadpoint, Stevens County

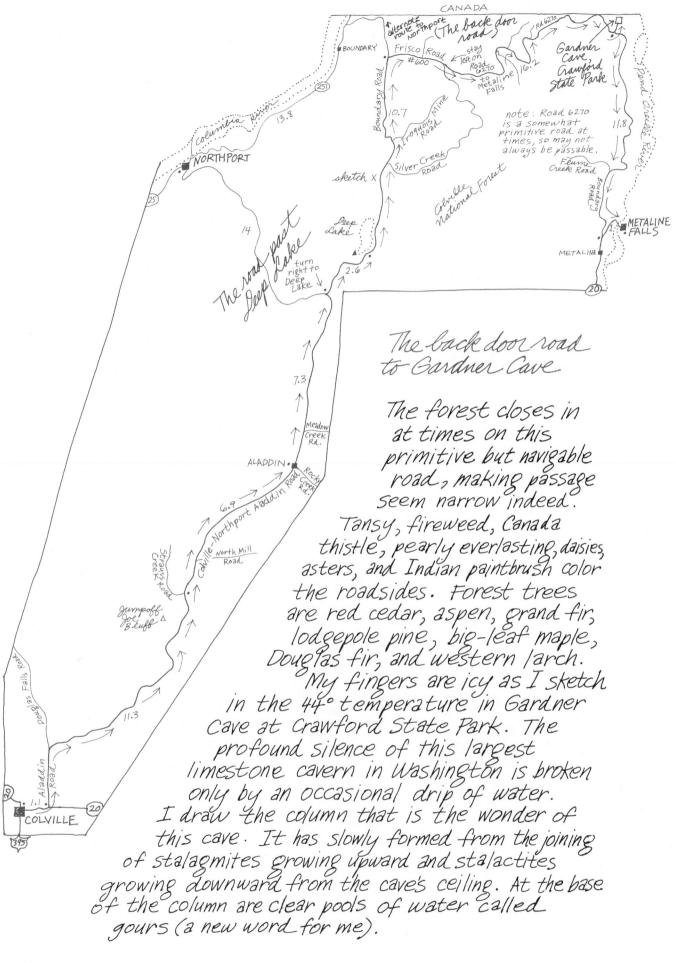

CANADA

alternate route to Northport (The back door road) Rd 6270

BOUNDARY

Frisco Road #600

stay left on Road 6270

to Metaline Falls

16.2

Gardner Cave Crawford State Park

Boundary Road

10.7

Iroquois Mine Road

Silver Creek Road

note: Road 6270 is a somewhat primitive road at times, so may not always be passable.

Colville National Forest

Pend Oreille River

11.8

Flume Creek Road

Boundary Road

METALINE FALLS

25¹

Columbia River

13.8

NORTHPORT

25

sketch X

Deep Lake

14

The road past Deep Lake

turn right to Deep Lake

2.6

METALINE

METALINE FALLS

20

7.3

Meadow Creek Rd.

ALADDIN

Rocky Creek Rd.

6.9

Colville-Northport Aladdin Road

North Mill Road

Strauss Creek Road

Jumpoff Joe B. Cliff

Douglas Falls Road

11.3

Aladdin Road

1.1

20

COLVILLE

20

395

The back door road to Gardner Cave

The forest closes in at times on this primitive but navigable road, making passage seem narrow indeed. Tansy, fireweed, Canada thistle, pearly everlasting, daisies, asters, and Indian paintbrush color the roadsides. Forest trees are red cedar, aspen, grand fir, lodgepole pine, big-leaf maple, Douglas fir, and western larch.

My fingers are icy as I sketch in the 44° temperature in Gardner Cave at Crawford State Park. The profound silence of this largest limestone cavern in Washington is broken only by an occasional drip of water.

I draw the column that is the wonder of this cave. It has slowly formed from the joining of stalagmites growing upward and stalactites growing downward from the cave's ceiling. At the base of the column are clear pools of water called gours (a new word for me).

Gardner Cave
near Metal
Pend Oreille County

147

Road to Manresa Grotto

From Metaline Falls, the road runs through forests, hugging the edge of the deep blue water of Sullivan Lake and south of Ione following the picturesque Pend Oreille River.
At Manresa Grotto, on the Kalispel Indian Reservation, I sketch the cool gray interior of this natural cathedral formed by solid rock. Established by Catholic priest Father Dement, it is a place that inspires worship and meditation, and was revered by the Kalispel Indian tribe (despite hard rock seats).

Manresa Grotto,
Pend Oreille County

149

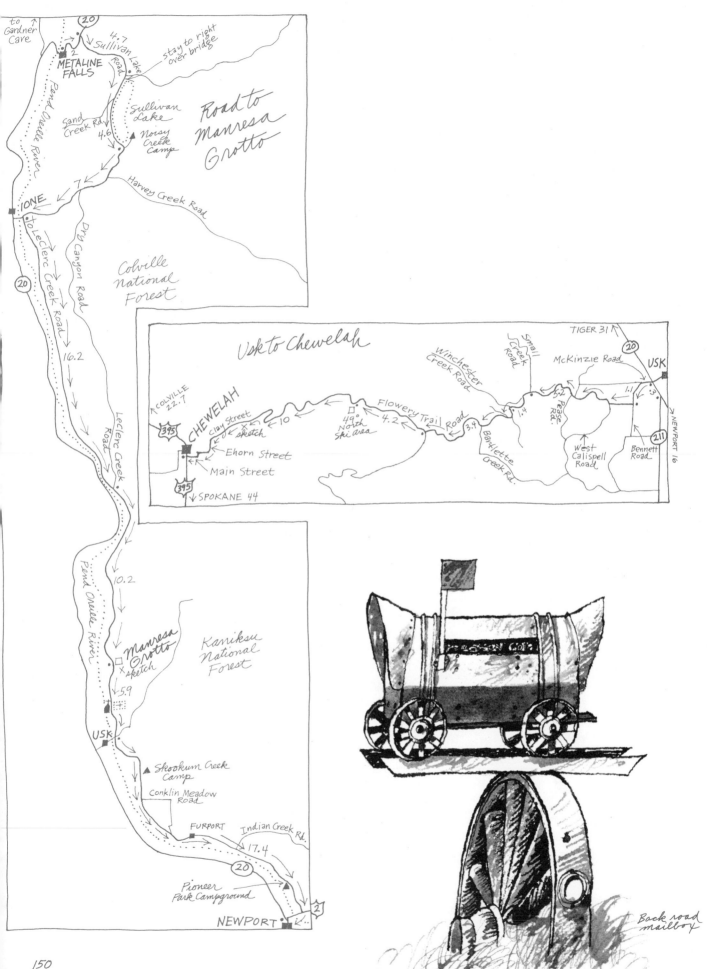

Road to Manresa Grotto

Usk to Chewelah

Back road mailbox

Back road
musician

151

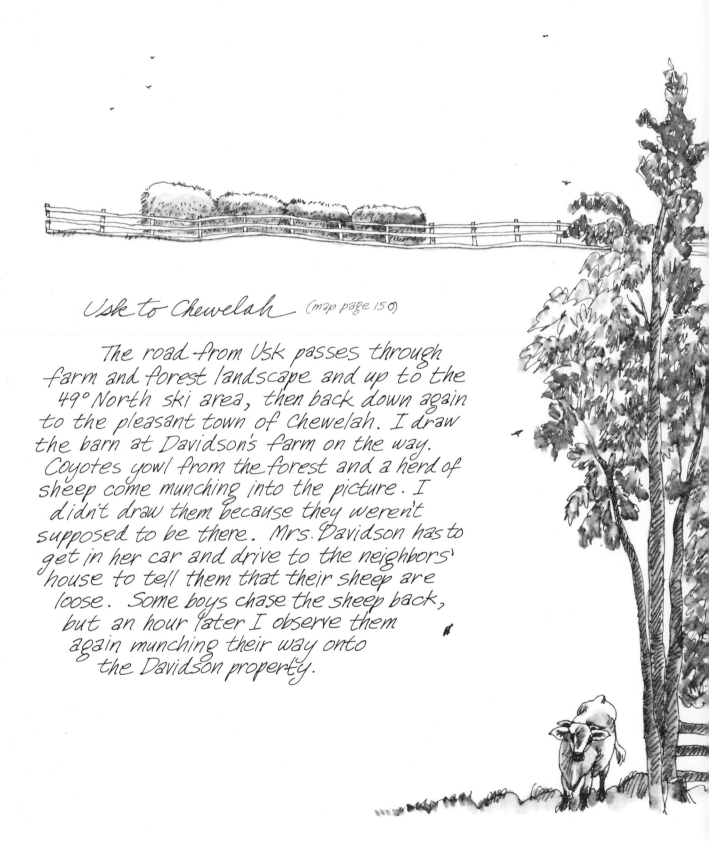

Usk to Chewelah (map page 150)

The road from Usk passes through farm and forest landscape and up to the 49° North ski area, then back down again to the pleasant town of Chewelah. I draw the barn at Davidson's farm on the way. Coyotes yowl from the forest and a herd of sheep come munching into the picture. I didn't draw them because they weren't supposed to be there. Mrs. Davidson has to get in her car and drive to the neighbors' house to tell them that their sheep are loose. Some boys chase the sheep back, but an hour later I observe them again munching their way onto the Davidson property.

Davidson's Farm
near Chewelah,
Stevens County

Back road through Colville Valley

There is great agricultural beauty to behold along this interesting back road — the patterns and textures of the crops, the sweeping lines of agricultural divisions. My reward for sitting quietly as I draw this farm scene is a magnificent, multicolored dragonfly that perches on my drawing board. I am extremely pleased to have inspired confidence in such an elegant member of the insect world.

*Ranch in Colville Valley,
Stevens County*

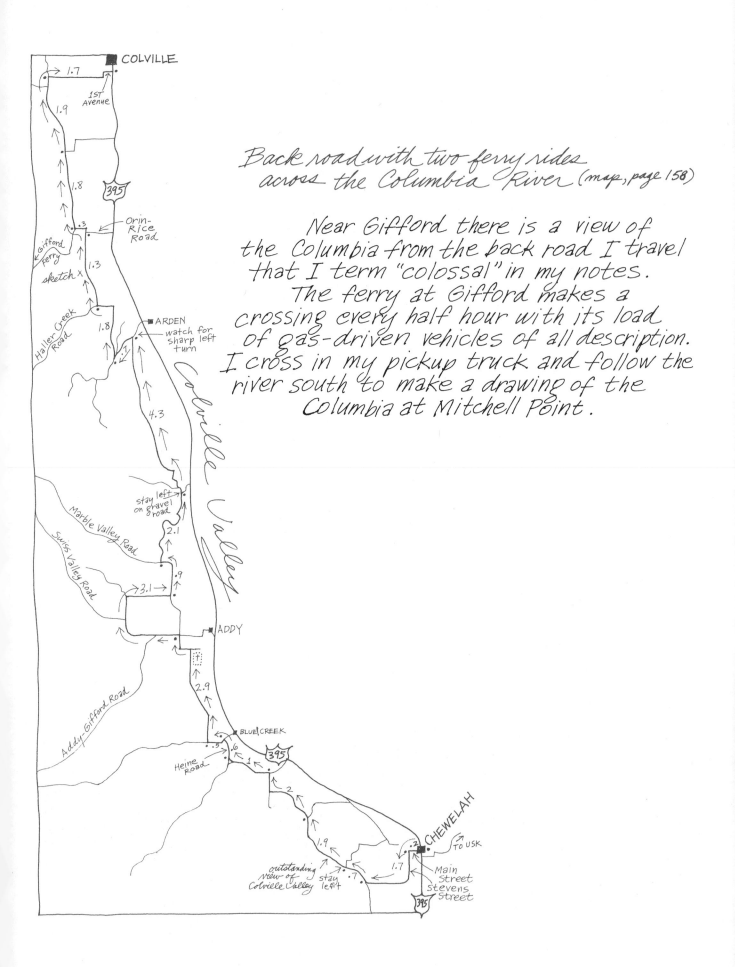

Back road with two ferry rides across the Columbia River (map, page 158)

Near Gifford there is a view of the Columbia from the back road I travel that I term "colossal" in my notes. The ferry at Gifford makes a crossing every half hour with its load of gas-driven vehicles of all description. I cross in my pickup truck and follow the river south to make a drawing of the Columbia at Mitchell Point.

The Columbia River,
Mitchell Point,
Colville Indian Reservation,
Ferry County

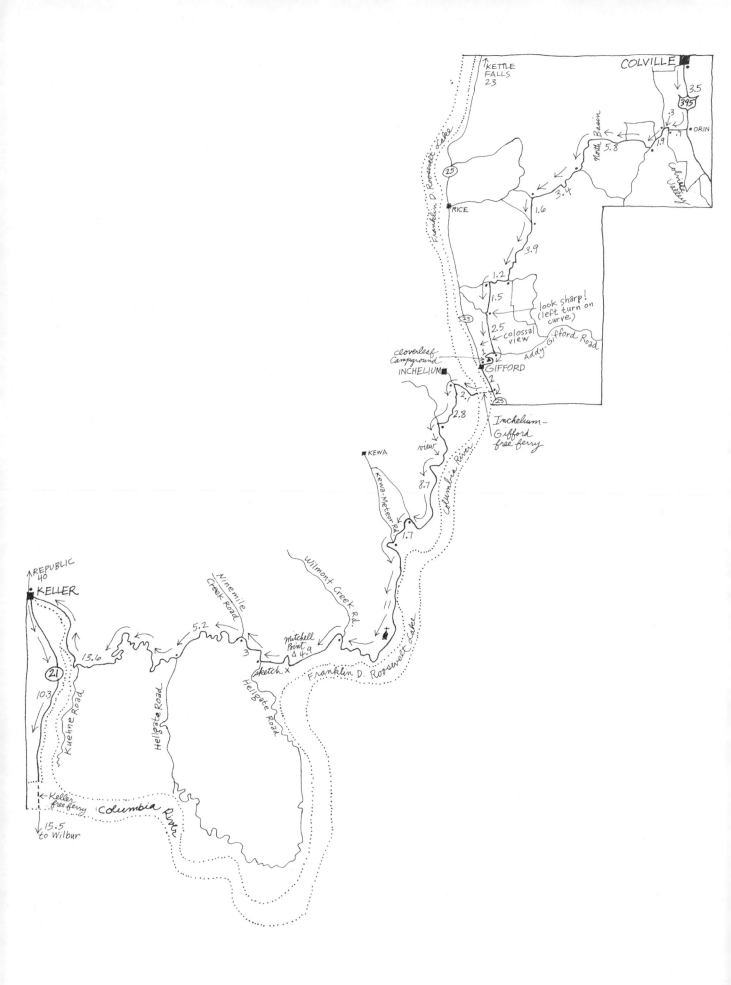

KETTLE
FALLS
23

COLVILLE

3.5

395

3

.7 • ORIN

.1.9

North Basin

5.8

3.4

1.6

Franklin D. Roosevelt Lake

25

• RICE

3.9

1.2

1.5

look sharp!
(left turn on
curve)

2.5
colossal
view

25

Addy–Gifford Road

Colville Valley

cloverleaf
Campground
INCHELIUM

GIFFORD

2.1

2.8

view

8.7

Columbia River

Inchelium–
Gifford
free ferry

• KEWA

Kewa–Meteor Rd.

1.7

Wilmont Creek Rd.

11

REPUBLIC
40

KELLER

Ninemile Creek Road

5.2

13.6

21

10.3

Kuehne Road

Hellgate Road

3

Hellgate Road

mitchell
Point
△ 4.9

sketch ✗

Franklin D. Roosevelt Lake

Keller
free ferry
Columbia River

15.5
to Wilbur

The Keller ferry ride at the end
of the back road trip through Colville
Indian country is delightful. I take
it four times in order to make the
drawing. During the eleven years
two operators worked the ferry,
bad weather halted its operation
on only one occasion. They
like their job but admit it
could be a bitterly cold crossing
in midwinter.

"Martha S," the ferry
across Columbia River,
Ferry and Lincoln Counties

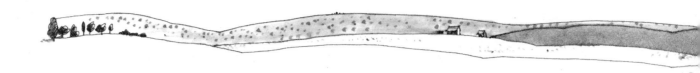

The road to Hartline

From Grand Coulee the road
winds through a rocky, sagebrush-covered
draw. There is a large view of Grand
Coulee dam, then a great rolling
landscape plateau of wheatland all
around. The horizon line is broken
here and there by a lone barn,
farm, and windmill and by an
old silo like this one sketched near
the grain elevator town
of Hartline.

Back road
mailbox

Old silo near Hartline, Grant County

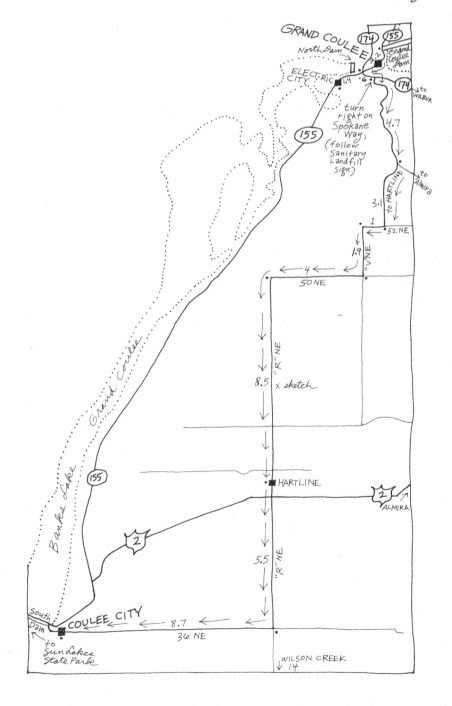

GRAND COULEE

North Dam

174   155

Grand Coulee Dam

ELECTRIC CITY   1.4   6   174   to WILBUR

turn right on Spokane Way; (follow Sanitary Landfill sign)

155   4.7   to Almira

to HARTLINE   3.1

1   52 NE

1.9   "J" NE

←4←   50 NE

"R" NE

8.5   × sketch

Banks Lake   Grand Coulee

155   ■ HARTLINE   2   ALMIRA

2   5.5   "R" NE

South Dam   COULEE CITY   ←8.7←   36 NE

to Sun Lakes State Parks   WILSON CREEK ↓14

Back road loop from Coulee City

To irrigate the farmlands of Washington, Summer Falls charges over this parapet of stone with thundering force. A hydroelectric generating facility will be placed here, a nearby notice reads. It may mean that the Falls will be eliminated, but in the meantime it is exciting to witness all that water seething, roiling, roaring, booming into Billy Clapp Lake.

The cliffs and sagebrush of Dry Coulee Road bring to mind scenery from movies of the Old West.

At Wilson Creek, where Zack Finney started the first school in 1892, and where an immigrant train arrived from Minnesota in 1901, there is a lovely shaded park just perfect for a picnic.

COULEE CITY

17 2

⬚ Dry Falls Park

SOAP LAKE

8.7

Leave Coulee City
at Main and
McEntee Streets
on Pinto Ridge
Road to Summer Falls.

8.7 ← 36 NE ← ←
← to HARTLINE

Summer Falls

Dry Coulee Road   .1 • 1.3
6.7   X sketch

Billy Coyote Lake

Brook Lake

14

"R" Road to Hartline

3

28   ⬚ STRATFORD

1.3 .5 ■ WILSON CREEK

6.4
22 NE

1.8

ADRIAN
1 → → 5 → →
20 NE

"J" NE

2

MARLIN →

28

to
ODESSA

Summer Falls,
Grant County

Roadside
sunflower,
Stevens County

164

Road along the Spokane River

The Spokane Indian reservation road cuts through pine forest and meadow. Now I drive along the Spokane River itself and enjoy a landscape of green crops, river views, occasional farms, and roadside sunflowers in abundance.

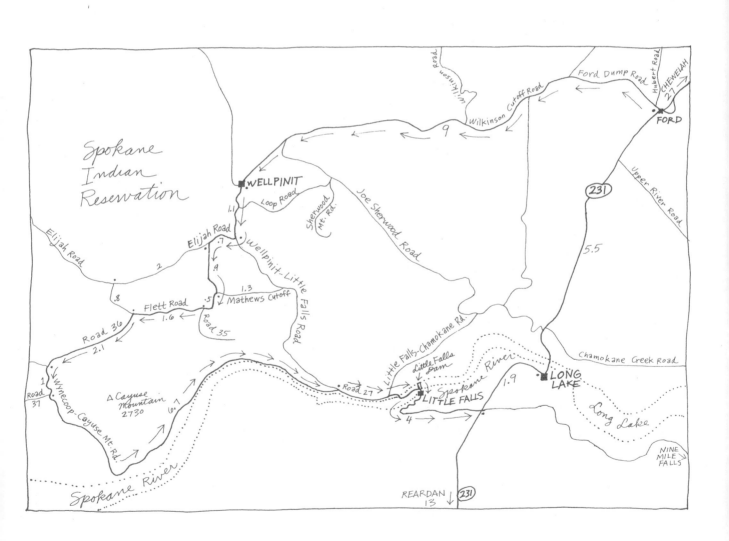

Dalmatian
Toadflax,
Spokane
County

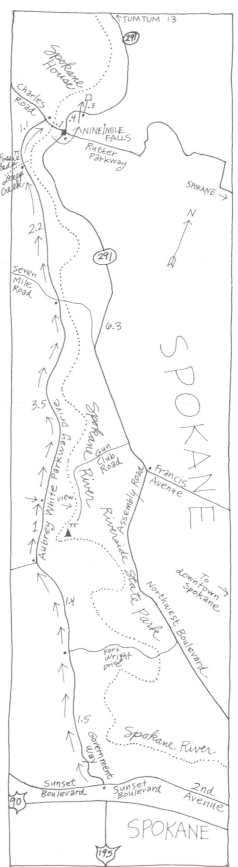

↑ TUMTUM 13

291

Spokane
House

Charles
Road

.3

.4

1.1

⚑ NINE MILE
FALLS

Rutter
Parkway

SPOKANE →

Fossil
Beds
Deep
Creek

N ↑

2.2

Seven
Mile
Road

291

6.3

S P O K A N E

3.5

Spokane Gun Club Road

Francis
Avenue

Aubrey White Parkway

Spokane River

view

1

Assembly Road

Riverside State Park

To
downtown
Spokane
→

Northwest Boulevard

1.4

Fort
Wright
Drive

1.5

Government Way

Spokane River

Sunset
Boulevard

Sunset
Boulevard

2nd
Avenue

90

SPOKANE

195

The road through Riverside State Park

There is a splendid view of Spokane from the ridge along this forest and river road. I explore Deep Creek Canyon and find a variety of wild flowers. I make studies of two common tansy, with its bright yellow flower heads resembling golden buttons, and a yellow flower with the incredible name of Dalmatian toadflax. Spokane House Interpretive Center can be visited at the end of the trip. It is the site of an 1810 trading post and the first permanent white settlement in Washington.

Tansy, Spokane County

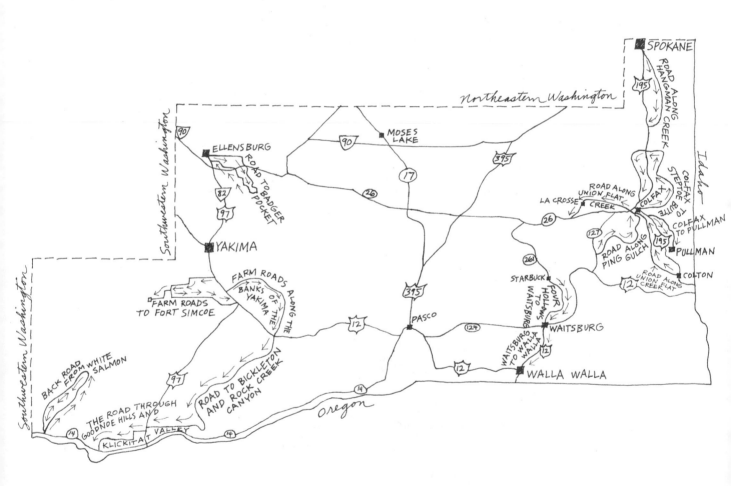

SPOKANE

Northeastern Washington

Southwestern Washington

Idaho

195 ROAD ALONG HANGMAN CREEK

90

ELLENSBURG

90 MOSES LAKE

395

17

ROAD TO BADGER POCKET

82

97

26

COLFAX STEPTOE BUTTE

ROAD ALONG UNION FLAT CREEK

LA CROSSE

COLFAX

COLFAX TO PULLMAN

YAKIMA

26

127

ROAD ALONG PING GULCH

195

PULLMAN

FARM ROADS ALONG THE BANKS OF THE YAKIMA

261

COLTON

ROAD ALONG UNION FLAT CREEK FLAT

2

FARM ROADS TO FORT SIMCOE

STARBUCK

FOUR HOLLOWS TO WAITSBURG

395

BACK ROAD FROM WHITE SALMON

12

PASCO

124

WAITSBURG

97

ROAD TO BICKLETON AND ROCK CREEK CANYON

WAITSBURG TO WALLA WALLA

12

12

THE ROAD THROUGH GOODNOE HILLS AND KLICKITAT VALLEY

14

14

WALLA WALLA

Southwestern Washington

14

Oregon

Southeastern Washington

I recall the fruit trees, grapevines,
and the tall green of hops in
Yakima Valley; the peas,
asparagus, and sweet onion
fields of Walla Walla;
the dairy and grain
country around Ellensburg,
and the rolling
wheatlands south of
Spokane. And in
late summer there is
the drama of the
harvest. By
traveling the back
roads, I witness
the great
agricultural
achievement of
the land.

Giant Blazing Star
(bright yellow flowers),
Klickitat County

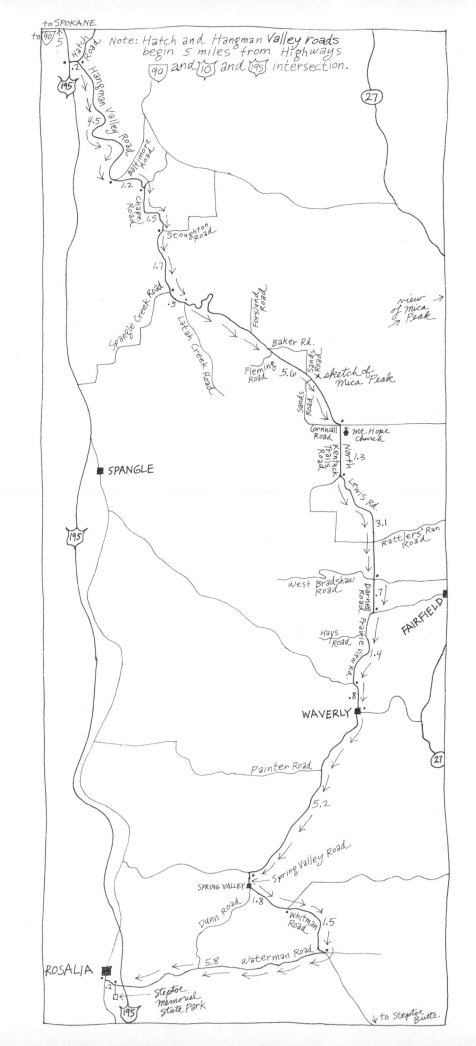

to SPOKANE

to 90 5

Hatch Road

.2

195

Note: Hatch and Hangman Valley roads begin 5 miles from Highways 90 and 10 and 195 intersection.

27

Hangman Valley Road

4.5

Baltimore Road

1.2

Chapel Road

1.5

Stoughton Road

1.7

Spangle Creek Road

.5

Latah Creek Road

Forslund Road

view of Mica Peak

Baker Rd.

Fleming Road

5.6

Sands Road

Perry Road

sketch of Mica Peak

Cornwall Road

Sands Road

Mt. Hope Church

Kentuck Trails Road

North

1.3

SPANGLE

Lewis Rd.

195

3.1

Rattlers' Run Road

West Bradshaw Road

Darnell Road

.7

FAIRFIELD

Hays Road

Prairie View Rd.

1.4

.8

WAVERLY

Painter Road

27

5.2

Spring Valley Road

SPRING VALLEY

Dunn Road

1.8

Whitman Road

1.5

ROSALIA

5.8

Waterman Road

.2

Steptoe Memorial State Park

195

to Steptoe Butte

The road along Hangman Creek

Hangman Creek Road soon brings me to the rolling grain and grass seed fields south of Spokane. From one vista point I sketch Mica Peak and the extensive agricultural land surrounding it. Bluegrass fields are being burned in the distance, the smoke threatening the visibility of the mountain. The sound of harvesting machinery fills the air from beyond the nearby hills.

Harvester,
Spokane County

172

Mica Peak,
Spokane County

Road along Ping Gulch

From the campground along the Snake River at Central Ferry I see tugs pushing loaded barges. They carry oil, grain, fish, and wood—a variety of products from Idaho. An incredibly long freight train creaks over a trestle suspended high above the Snake. An image of Buster Keaton racing and leaping from car to car comes to mind. I am occupied counting cars for quite a while, for it turns out there are a hundred of them!

In Ping Gulch there are cows, rolling wheatlands, creekside willows, roadside sunflowers, neat farmhouses, and dogs running alongside my vehicle.

Ping Gulch ranch,
Garfield County

At Lower Granite Lock and Dam on the Snake River
I visit the Fish Viewing Room and the fish ladder. There
are steelhead trout, channel catfish, carp, salmon, and
many other fish to see.
    The hills roll gracefully on either side of the
road to Colfax. I feel that I am gaining more
knowledge of the land and its farming people
for taking this meandering series of back
    country roads.

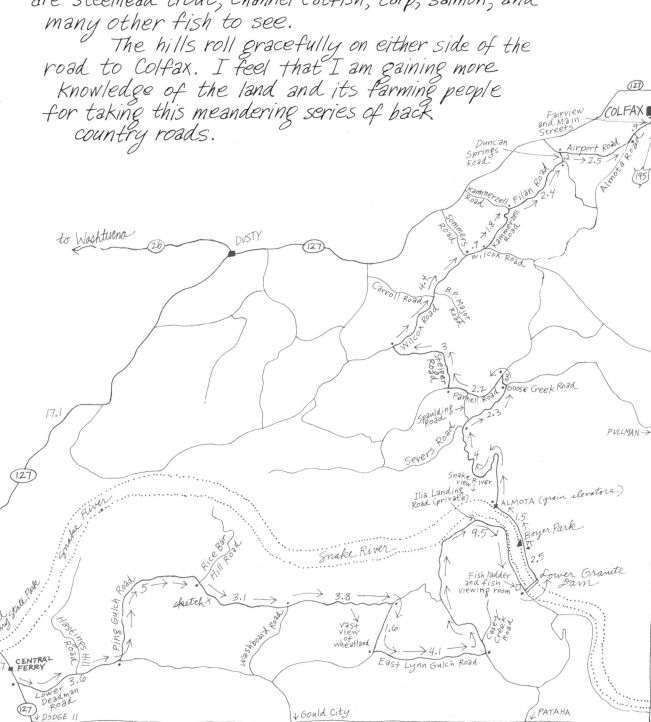

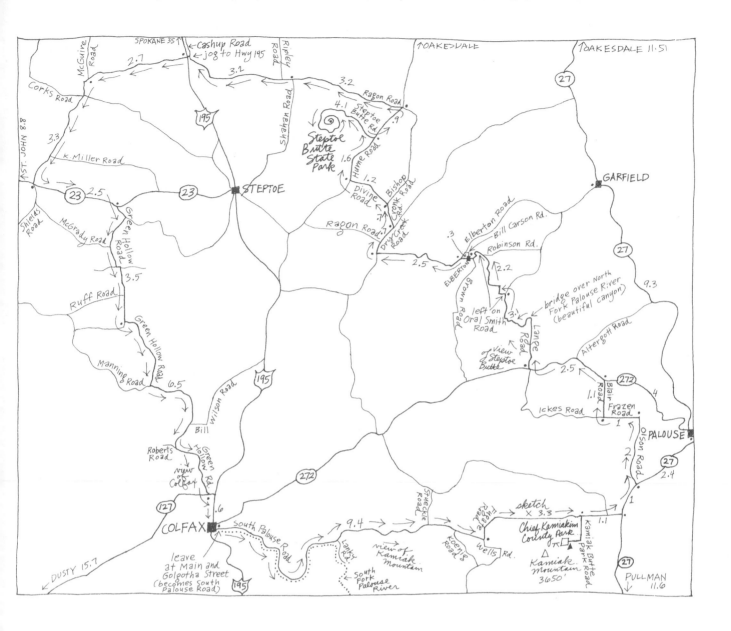

Colfax to Steptoe Butte

I follow the Palouse River past well-kept farmhouses, their gardens adorned with flowers. Near Kamiak Butte I make a drawing of the rolling farmland. Kamiak was a famous Yakima Indian chieftain, and the butte named after him is now a county park. I cross the Palouse River, here flowing through a deep canyon, and proceed to the picturesque community of Elberton. Later, as I appreciate the view from atop Steptoe Butte, I reflect on the geology of this region. I am looking down from an ancient mountain that ten million years ago was

Surrounded by lava
flows. Kamiak Butte
is another old
mountain that lava
had surrounded but
not covered. The
rich covering of
dirt and topsoil,
layered over the old
lava flows, today
support the Palouse
area's large-scale
dry farming of
peas, lentils, and wheat.

Landscape near Colfax,
Whitman County

Country road from Colfax to Pullman

In Colfax, on Perkins Avenue near Last Street, you can see the 1884 Victorian house of the first permanent resident of the town, James A. Perkins. (If you wish to see the interior, write to the Whitman County Historical Society, Box 447, Pullman.)

The farmland in this area was once covered with bunchgrass. Early settlers called it palouse, from the French word for short, thick grass.

In a quiet valley I sketch the McIntosh Angus Ranch red barn and house. The black angus pictured here is particularly clean, for it has just been washed by a member of the McIntosh family. Other back roads beckon me to the delightful university town of Pullman, at the junction of the three forks of the Palouse River.

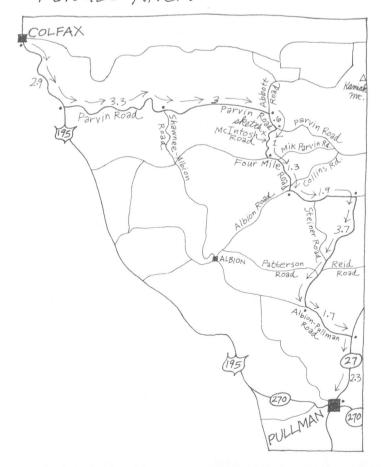

McIntosh Angus Ranch,
Whitman County

Union Flat Creek

Union Flat Creek Rd.

Jim Knott Road

Endicott SW Road

Union Flat Creek

15.6

Guske Road

Lone John Moraschi Rd.

Luft Road

Winona South Road

6.4

LA CROSSE

26

26

WASHTUCNA 21

Grain elevator,
Union Flat Creek Road,
Whitman County

The road along Union Flat Creek

I proceed through valley landscape past handsome farms and big barns. Willow trees grow along the creek. Klemgard County Park is situated on an attractive site for picnicking.

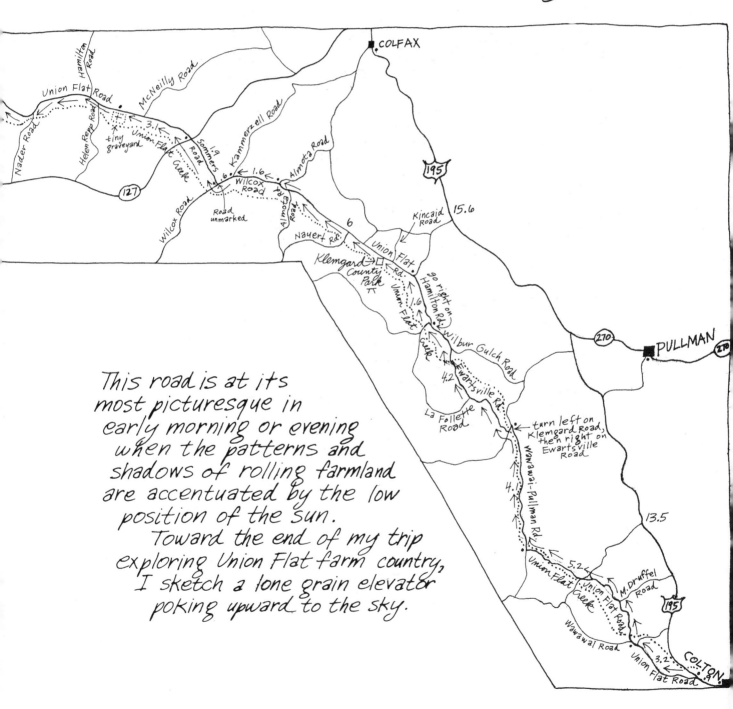

This road is at its most picturesque in early morning or evening when the patterns and shadows of rolling farmland are accentuated by the low position of the sun.

Toward the end of my trip exploring Union Flat farm country, I sketch a lone grain elevator poking upward to the sky.

1892 Drugstore,
Waitsburg
Walla Walla
County

Four Hollows to Waitsburg

South of Washtucna, Adams County, are two well-maintained state parks: Palouse Falls and Lyons Ferry. Crossing the Snake River at Lyons Ferry, I travel back roads with names like Smith Hollow, Whetstone Hollow, Thorn Hollow, Sorghum Hollow, and even Whoopemup Hollow.

Near Waitsburg, on Highway 12, is Lewis and Clark Trail State Park, where in May 1806, Lewis and Clark's party ate parsnips and dog meat, having nothing else to choose from. In historic Waitsburg I sketch two facades in the well-preserved old town. At the local newspaper, the _Times_, the editor informs me that the paper's 1888 building once had a decorative design at the top that has long since been removed. He suspects that the lawyer who used to have his office there had the peaked and turreted top taken off when the bricks and mortar began to show some wear. The lawyer, he conjectured, had been trying to avoid suit should a brick dislodge and fall on a passerby. However, the editor studied the prevailing wind direction, and it

The Times,
Waitsburg,
Walla
Walla
County

was his conclusion that should any part have deteriorated enough to fall, it would have fallen in the direction of the roof, not the street. The missing top accounted for the building's rather blunt roof line.

J.W. Morgan's 1892 drugstore has today been put to another use, but the well-proportioned, early Waitsburg design is still almost intact. Testimony to Waitsburg's interest in preserving its heritage of history is the Bruce Memorial Museum, at 4th and Main streets, which should also be seen while you are in town.

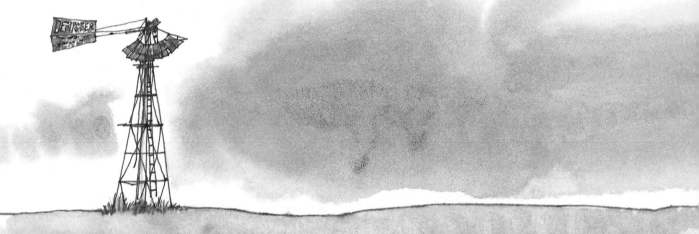

Waitsburg to Walla Walla

This road takes me through the agricultural land north of Walla Walla, then east of the city to the "walk-in entrance" of Whitman Mission. It is a peaceful place of great beauty, but it is also the site of the massacre of the missionary Marcus Whitman family and other mission members by Cayuse Indians in 1847. The Cayuse had their reasons: one of them was that white settlers visiting the mission had transmitted a measles epidemic to the Indians that had wiped out half their tribe! When a cure could not be found by missionary-doctor Whitman, the Indians lost faith in the Whitman cause. There is more to the dramatic story; it awaits you at the Whitman Mission.

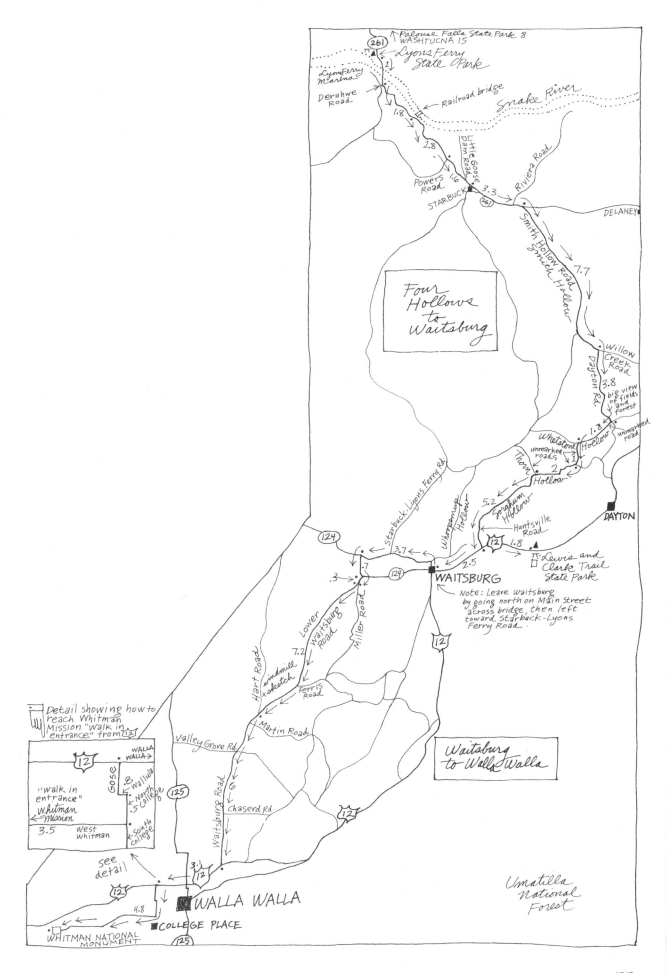

Palouse Falls State Park 8
WASHTUCNA 15

Lyons Ferry State Park

Lyons Ferry Marina

Deruhwe Road

Railroad bridge

Snake River

Little Goose Dam Road

Powers Road

STARBUCK

Riviera Road

DELANEY

Smith Hollow Road
Smith Hollow

Four Hollows to Waitsburg

Willow Creek Road

Dayton Rd.

big view of fields and forest

Whetstone Hollow
unmarked road

unmarked roads

Thorn Hollow

Sorghum Hollow

Whoopemup Hollow

Huntsville Road

DAYTON

Starbuck-Lyons Ferry Rd.

Lewis and Clark Trail State Park

WAITSBURG

Note: Leave Waitsburg by going north on Main Street across bridge, then left toward Starbuck-Lyons Ferry Road.

Lower Waitsburg Road

Miller Road

Hart Road

windmill ×sketch

Ferris Road

Waitsburg to Walla Walla

Detail showing how to reach Whitman Mission "walk in entrance" from 12

Martin Road

Valley Grove Rd.

Waitsburg Road

Chaserd Rd.

WALLA WALLA

Gose

Wallula

North College

South College

"walk in entrance"
Whitman Mission

West Whitman

see detail

Umatilla National Forest

WALLA WALLA

COLLEGE PLACE

WHITMAN NATIONAL MONUMENT

The road to Badger Pocket

Frail ninety-year-old Clareta Olmstead shows me
the old cottonwood log cabin built by the Olmstead
family in 1875. Its historic furnishings include an
1870 Scottish spinning wheel. It is now part of a
state park and is open to visitors most of the year.
There are many other turn-of-the-century buildings
in addition to the log cabin. As I sketch, peacocks
strut about the grounds occasionally giving off
plaintive, loud, babylike cries.

Olmstead Cabin, 1875,
Kittitas County

ELLENSBURG

90
CLE ELUM
23

Mt. View Road   4   #6 Road   2.2   KITTITAS

.8

821   .3

Berry Rd.

Bull Rd.   1.1

Tjossem Road   1.6

82

97

Squaw Creek Road   .8

Olmstead Cabin

90

4th Ave. and Main

Railroad Avenue   1.1

.4 Badger Pocket Road   1.3

Windy Road

Vantage

VANTAGE   21

90

VANTAGE

Tjossem Road   1.3

Moe Road

Ferguson Rd.   2.1

Cleman Road

Carroll Road   1.4

Prater Road   1.2

Sorenson Road   Emerson Road   1.3

Billiter Rd.   2.5

Badger Pocket Rd.

Oda Johnson Rd.

Hamilton Road   1

E. Larsen Road   1

Badger   Badger   Pocket   Road

Boch Road   1   A. Larsen Road

Bare Rd.   1

Thrall Road   Les Wilson Rd.

Denmark Road

4th Parallel Rd.   Xsketch   5.5   4th Parallel Road   .9

B. Clerf Road   1.1   Ditchbanks Road   Morrison Rd.   .5

Ross Rd.   1

Manastash Ridge

821

Katen Rd.   W. Pt. Rd.   Katen Rd.   Badger Pocket Road   Borland Road   Bynum Rd.   .6   Hayes Road   1

Dead end

YAKIMA   YAKIMA 32

Badger Pocket landscape,
near Ellensburg, Kittitas County

Following this visit I explore Badger Pocket, where green farmland pushes up into the sagebrush-covered surrounding hills. This is rich dairyland, and green and golden hay crops and Hereford cattle are in plenitude.

Ellensburg, called Robber's Roost in 1870, contains many historic buildings. You should obtain a map showing them at the Chamber of Commerce.

Farm roads to Fort Simcoe

Past apple and peach orchards, pastureland, fields of mint, corn, and hay, these roads finally lead to Fort Simcoe. Located on the Yakima Indian Reservation, the fort was originally built to oversee the Indians and to protect Yakima Treaty areas from land-hungry settlers.

I liked Fort Simcoe for its spacious lawns and venerable oaks. The Yakimas called the location Mool Mool, a place of bubbling springs.

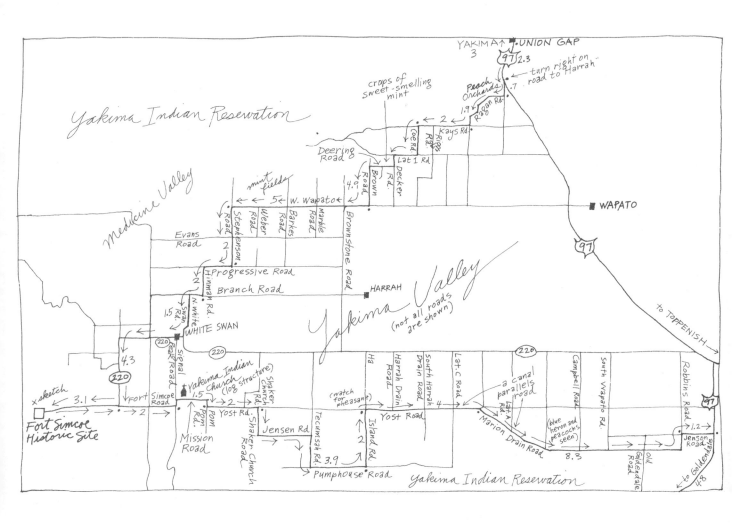

Yakima Indian Reservation

YAKIMA↑•UNION GAP
3
(97) 2.3
→ "turn right on road to Harrah"
.7

Peach Orchards
1.9← Ragan Rd.

crops of sweet-smelling mint

← 2
Coe Rd.
Kipps Rd.
Kays Rd.

Deering Road

Lat 1 Rd.
Decker Rd.
Brown Road
4.9

■ WAPATO

mint fields
← 5 W. Wapato ←

Medicine Valley

Stephenson Road
Weber Road
Barkes Road
Marble Road
Brownstone Road

Evans Road
2

1 Progressive Road
2
Inman Rd.
Branch Road

■ HARRAH

Yakima Valley
(not all roads are shown)

1.5
Swan Rd.
N. white

WHITE SWAN

(220)
Peak Road
Signal
(220)

4.3

(220)

x sketch
← 3.1 ←
Fort Simcoe Road
→ 2 →

Fort Simcoe Historic Site

† Yakima Indian Church (log structure)
1.5
Shaker Church Rd.
Yost Rd.
← 2 →

Pom Rd.
Pom Rd.

Mission Road

Shaker Church Road

Jensen Rd.
→

Tecumsah Rd.
3.9

← 2
Island Rd.

(watch for pheasant)

Yost Road

Ha
Harrah Drain Road
South Harrah Drain Road
Lat. C Road
← 4 →

a canal parallels road

Lat. A Rd.
Marion Drain Road
(blue heron and peacocks seen)
8.3

Campbell Road
South Wapato Rd.

Robbins Road

(220)

(97)

Goldendale Road
old
Jenson Road
→
← 1.2

→

to TOPPENISH →

↙ to Goldendale 48

→ Pumphouse Road   Yakima Indian Reservation

Fort Simcoe Historical Site,
Yakima County

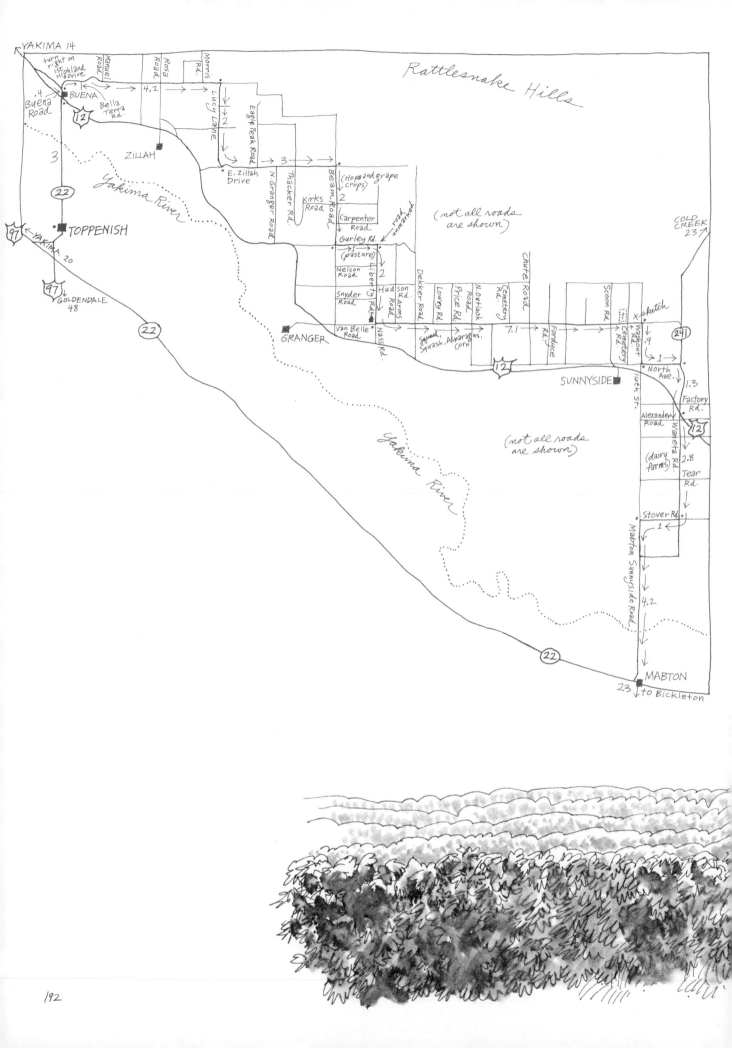

YAKIMA 14

turn right on 1st/Highland Drive

Manuel Road

Rosa Road

Morris Rd.

Rattlesnake Hills

.4
Buena Road

BUENA

Bella Terra Rd.

4.2

Lucy Lane

2

Eagle Peak Road

12

ZILLAH

3

22

Yakima River

E. Zillah Drive

N. Granger Road

Thacker Rd.

3

Beam Road

Kirks Road

(Hops and grape crops)

2

Carpenter Road

Gurley Rd.

road unmarked

(not all roads are shown)

COLD CREEK 23

97

YAKIMA

TOPPENISH

20

97

GOLDENDALE 48

22

1 (pasture)

Nelson Road

Liberty Rd.

2

Hudson Rms Rd.

Snyder Road

Dekker Road

Lowry Rd.

Price Rd.

N. Outlook Road

Cemetery Rd.

Chute Road

Scoon Rd.

x sketch

241

Van Belle Road

Nass Rd.

Squash, Squash, Asparagus, corn

7.1

Fordyce Rd.

Cemetery Rd.

Washout

.9

1

GRANGER

12

North Ave.

1.3

SUNNYSIDE

16th St.

Factory Rd.

Alexander Road

Waneta Rd.

12

(not all roads are shown)

(dairy farms)

2.8

Tear Rd.

Stover Rd.

1

Mabton Sunnyside Road

4.2

Yakima River

22

MABTON

23 to Bickleton

Farm roads along the banks of the Yakima

    Apples, plums, asparagus, corn, hops, and grapes are some of the crops that grow along these roads. Hops are derived from a most decorative plant that has green garlands of leaves ten to twenty feet high. I sketch a house seemingly engulfed by grapevines. Premium-quality grapes are grown in Yakima Valley for Washington's fine wines.
    Farm roads to Fort Simcoe and also this drive on the east bank of the Yakima River illustrate the agricultural abundance of the great Yakima Valley.

Vineyard near Sunnyside, Yakima County

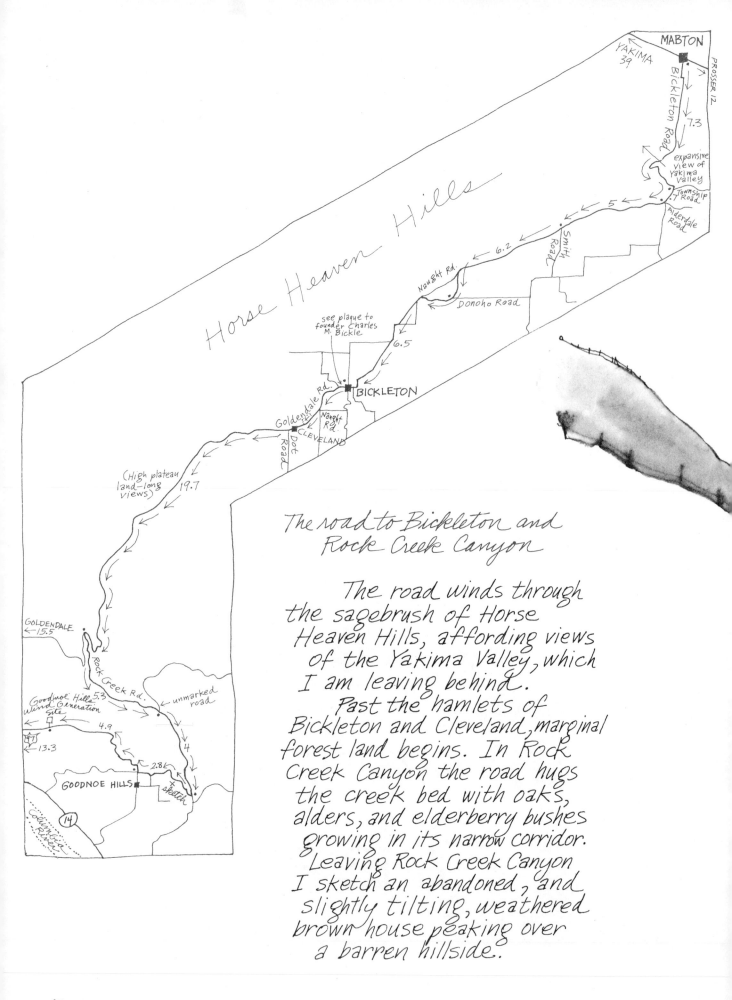

Horse Heaven Hills

MABTON

YAKIMA 39

PROSSER 12

Bickleton Road

7.3

expansive view of Yakima Valley

Township Road .7

Alderdale Road

5

Smith Road

6.2

Naught Rd.

Donoho Road

see plaque to founder Charles M. Bickle

6.5

Goldendale Rd.

BICKLETON

Naught Rd.

Dot Road

CLEVELAND

(High plateau land—long views)

19.7

GOLDENDALE
← 15.5

Rock Creek Rd.

Goodnoe Hills Wind Generation Site

5.3

unmarked road

97

4.9

← 13.3

4

2.8

GOODNOE HILLS

sketch

14

Columbia River

The road to Bickleton and
Rock Creek Canyon

The road winds through
the sagebrush of Horse
Heaven Hills, affording views
of the Yakima Valley, which
I am leaving behind.
Past the hamlets of
Bickleton and Cleveland, marginal
forest land begins. In Rock
Creek Canyon the road hugs
the creek bed with oaks,
alders, and elderberry bushes
growing in its narrow corridor.
Leaving Rock Creek Canyon
I sketch an abandoned, and
slightly tilting, weathered
brown house peaking over
a barren hillside.

Ghostly house, near
Rock Creek Canyon, Klickitat County

The road through Goodnoe Hills
and Klickitat Valley

Good views of Columbia River country are along these roads, including the big mountains Hood and Adams. I pass the Goodnoe Hills Wind Generation Site with three of the world's largest and most advanced wind turbine generators, and proceed into the broad Klickitat Valley where I sketch a lonely farm.

The Dalles Mountain Road begins here, a slow, bumpy road over the Columbia hills. Once over the ridge I come upon a view that I will never forget. I imagine that I am looking south over the whole state of Oregon, its agricultural patterns continuing to infinity. The road is an exciting one both for its wonderful views and for the thrill of its precipitous mountain drive.

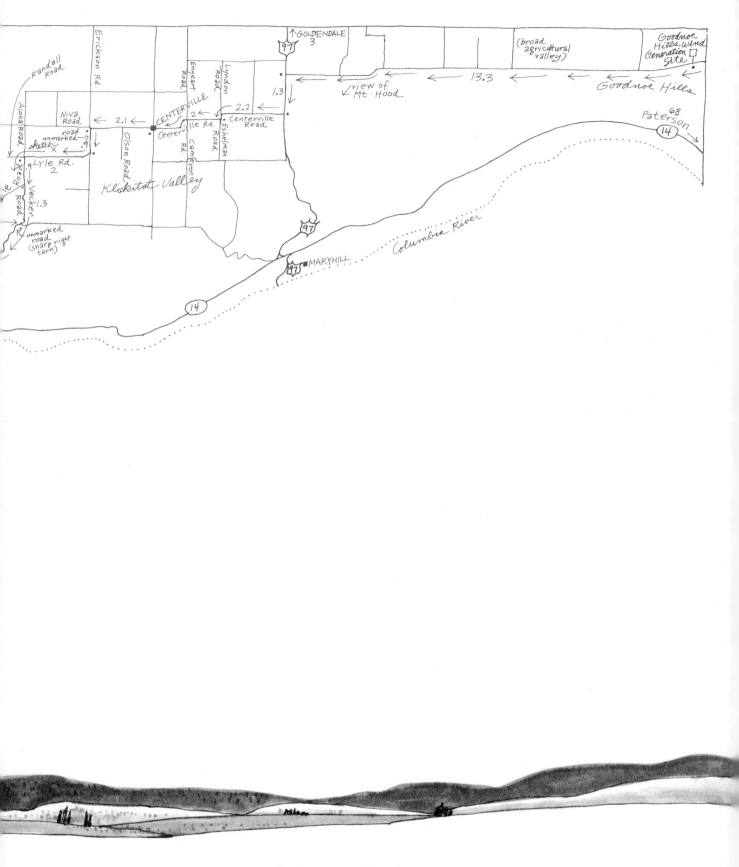

Klickitat Valley landscape, Klickitat County

View of Mount Adams,
near Glenwood,
Klickitat County

Back road from White Salmon

Mountain and forest views, green meadows and old farmhouses describe the landscape along this back road. Near Conboy Lake I sketch Mount Adams, a ghostly old farmhouse in the foreground. Glenwood is a lively little town to visit; then I drive toward BZ Corners where I observe the pleasant dairy countryside with its cows, hay crops, and big old barns.
It is a good road to end my memorable journey through the beautiful state of Washington.

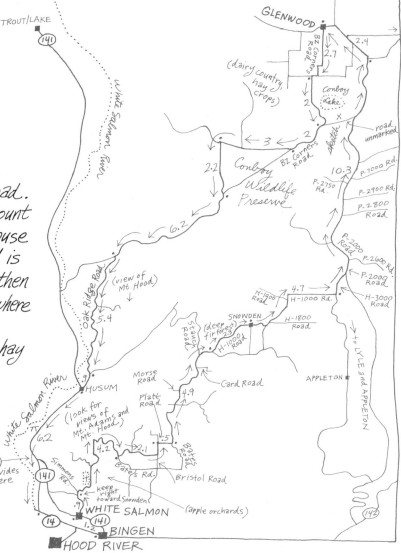

TROUT LAKE

141

GLENWOOD

to GOLDENDALE

BZ Corners Road

2.4

2.7

(dairy country, hay crops)

Conboy Lake

2

road unmarked

White Salmon River

2

2

BZ Corners Road

sketch

X

10.3

P-7000 Rd.

2.2

Conboy Wildlife Preserve

P-2750 Rd.

P-2900 Rd.

P-2800 Road

6.2

P-2000 Road

P-2600 Rd.

P-200a Road

Oak Ridge Road

(view of Mt. Hood)

4.7

H-1000 Rd.

H-3000 Road

H-1900 Road

5.4

SNOWDEN

H-1800 Road

(deep fir forest)

Starch Road

2.3

H-1000 Road

Morse Road

Card Road

APPLETON

.9

HUSUM

4.9

to LYLE and APPLETON

White Salmon River

(look for views of Mt. Adams and Mt. Hood)

Platt Road

6.2

4.2

2.1

.5

Bates Road

141 divides here

Simmons Rd.

141

Bates Rd.

Bristol Road

keep right toward Snowden

.9

WHITE SALMON

(apple orchards)

14

1.2

141

BINGEN

HOOD RIVER

142

199

Epilogue

It is my wish that road builders will not straighten and widen our most picturesque back roads. And not even take out all the bumps. It encourages motorists to go ever faster, and to spend less time enjoying the trip. I agree that there must be fast highways and other fast roads, but there are also other roads that need not be.

As an artist, I am particularly concerned with impressions of nature, farmland and architecture. To make each day a series of remembered aesthetic experiences seems to me a happy goal.

As my respect for my fellowman makes me proud to be human, so my respect for nature makes me proud to be part of it.

I wish you many happy travels.

Frog Rock, Bainbridge Island, Kitsap County

Log corral, Medicine Valley, Yakima County

Thanks to artist Joe Seney and son Wes Thollander for their good company on portions of the 6000-mile back road trip through Washington.

200